# MAN

MAN IN THE FICTIONAL MODE   Books 1–6

MAN IN THE DRAMATIC MODE   Books 1–6

MAN IN THE POETIC MODE   Books 1–6

MAN IN THE EXPOSITORY MODE   Books 1–6

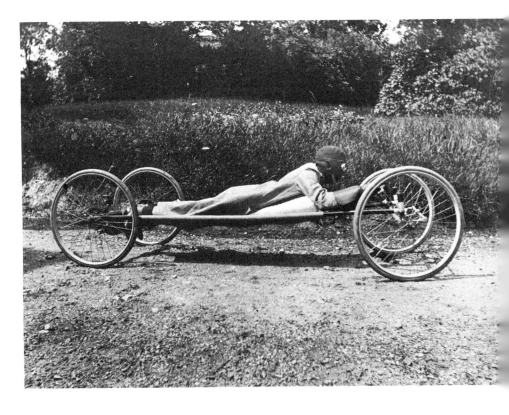

# MAN IN THE EXPOSITORY MODE

editor **Sarah Solotaroff**

**ries consultant  Geoffrey Summerfield**

torial direction  Joy Zweigler
sign  W. C. Bright
to consultation  James Newberry

**McDOUGAL, LITTELL & COMPANY**
Evanston, Illinois

Acknowledgments: Charles Scribner's Sons: For ''Bull Fighting a Tragedy,'' reprinted by permission of Charles Scribner's Sons from *By-Line: Ernest Hemingway,* edited by William White. Copyright © 1967 By-Line Ernest Hemingway, Inc.

E. P. Dutton & Co., Inc.: For a selection from *Time Is Short and the Water Rises* by John Walsh and Robert Gannon. Copyright © 1967 by International Society for the Protection of Animals. (continued on page 137)

# Contents

# MASCOT
## MALCOLM X

On June twenty-seventh of that year, nineteen thirty-seven, Joe Louis knocked out James J. Braddock to become the heavyweight champion of the world. And all the Negroes in Lansing, like Negroes everywhere, went wildly happy with the greatest celebration of race pride our generation had ever known. Every Negro boy old enough to walk wanted to be the next Brown Bomber. My brother Philbert, who had already become a pretty good boxer in school, was no exception. (I was trying to play basketball. I was gangling and tall, but I wasn't very good at it— too awkward.) In the fall of that year, Philbert entered the amateur bouts that were held in Lansing's Prudden Auditorium.

He did well, surviving the increasingly tough eliminations. I would go down to the gym and watch him train. It was very exciting. Perhaps without realizing it I became secretly envious; for one thing, I know I could not help seeing some of my younger brother Reginald's lifelong admiration for me getting siphoned off to Philbert.

People praised Philbert as a natural boxer. I figured that since we belonged to the same family, maybe I would become one, too. So I put myself in the ring. I think I was thirteen when I signed up for my first bout, but my height and rawboned frame let me get away with claiming that I was sixteen, the minimum age—and my weight of about 128 pounds got me classified as a bantamweight.

They matched me with a white boy, a novice like myself, named Bill Peterson. I'll never forget him. When our turn in the next amateur bouts came up, all of my brothers and sisters were there watching, along with just about everyone else I knew in town. They were there not so much because of me but because of Philbert, who had begun to build up a pretty good following, and they wanted to see how his brother would do.

I walked down the aisle between the people thronging the rows of seats, and climbed in the ring. Bill Peterson and I were introduced, and then the referee called us together and mumbled all of that stuff about fighting fair and breaking clean. Then the bell rang and we came out of our corners. I knew I was scared, but I didn't know, as Bill Peterson told me later on, that he was scared of me, too. He was so scared I was going to hurt him that he knocked me down fifty times if he did once.

He did such a job on my reputation in the Negro neighborhood that I practically went into hiding. A Negro just can't be whipped by somebody white and return with his head up to the neighborhood, especially in those days, when sports and, to a lesser extent show business, were the only fields open to Negroes, and when the ring was the only place a Negro could whip a white man and not be lynched. When I did show my face again, the Negroes I knew rode me so badly I knew I had to do something.

But the worst of my humiliations was my younger brother Reginald's attitude: he simply never mentioned the fight. It was the way he looked at me—and avoided looking at me. So I went back to the gym, and I trained—hard. I beat bags and skipped rope and grunted and sweated all over the place. And finally I signed up to fight Bill Peterson again. This time, the bouts were held in his hometown of Alma, Michigan.

The only thing better about the rematch was that hardly anyone I knew was there to see it; I was particularly grateful for Reginald's absence. The moment the bell rang, I saw a fist, then the canvas coming up, and ten seconds later the referee was saying *"Ten!"* over me. It was probably the shortest "fight" in history. I lay there listening to the full count, but I couldn't move. To tell the truth, I'm not sure I wanted to move.

That white boy was the beginning and the end of my fight career. A lot of times in these later years since I became a Muslim, I've thought back to that fight and reflected that it was Allah's work to stop me: I might have wound up punchy.

Not long after this, I came into a classroom with my hat on. I did it deliberately. The teacher, who was white, ordered me to keep the hat on, and to walk around and around the room until he told me to stop. "That way," he said, "everyone can see you. Meanwhile, we'll go on with class for those who are here to learn something."

I was still walking around when he got up from his desk and turned to the blackboard to write something on it. Everyone in the classroom was looking when, at this moment, I passed behind his desk, snatched up a thumbtack and deposited it in his chair. When he turned to sit back down, I was far from the scene of the crime, circling around the rear of the room. Then he hit the tack, and I heard him holler and caught a glimpse of him spraddling up as I disappeared through the door.

With my deportment record, I wasn't really shocked when the decision came that I had been expelled.

I guess I must have had some vague idea that if I didn't have to go to school, I'd be allowed to stay on with the Gohannas and wander around town, or maybe get a job if I wanted one for pocket money. But I got rocked on my heels when a state man whom I hadn't seen before came and got me at the Gohannas and took me down to court.

They told me I was going to go to a reform school. I was still thirteen years old.

But first I was going to the detention home. It was in Mason, Michigan, about twelve miles from Lansing. The detention home was where all the "bad" boys and girls from Ingham County were held, on their way to reform school—waiting for their hearings.

The white state man was a Mr. Maynard Allen. He was nicer to me than most of the state Welfare people had been. He even had consoling words for the Gohannas and Mrs. Adcock and Big Boy; all of them were crying. But I wasn't. With the few clothes I owned stuffed into a box, we rode in his car to Mason. He talked as he drove along, saying that my school marks showed that if I would just straighten up, I could make something of myself. He said that reform school had the wrong reputation; he talked about what the word "reform" meant —to change and become better. He said the school was really a place where boys like me could have time to see their mistakes and start a new life and become somebody everyone would be proud of. And he told me that the lady in charge of the detention home, a Mrs. Swerlin, and her husband were very good people.

They were good people. Mrs. Swerlin was bigger than her husband, I remember, a big, buxom, robust, laughing woman, and Mr. Swerlin was thin, with black hair, and a black mustache and a red face, quiet and polite, even to me.

They liked me right away, too. Mrs. Swerlin showed me to my room, my own room—the first in my life. It was in one of those huge dormitory-like buildings where kids in detention were kept in those days—and still are in most places. I discovered next, with surprise, that I was allowed to eat with the Swerlins. It was the first time I'd eaten with white people—at least with grown white people—since the Seventh Day Adventist country meetings. It wasn't my own exclusive privilege, of course. Except for the very troublesome boys and girls at the detention home, who were kept locked up—those who had run away and been caught and brought back, or something like that—all of us ate with the Swerlins sitting at the head of the long tables.

They had a white cook-helper, I recall—Lucille Lathrop. (It amazes me how these names come back, from a time I haven't thought about for more than twenty years.) Lucille treated me well, too. Her husband's name was Duane Lathrop. He worked somewhere else, but he stayed there at the detention home on the weekends with Lucille.

I noticed again how white people smelled different from us, and how their food tasted different, not seasoned like Negro cooking. I began to sweep and mop and dust around in the Swerlins' house, as I had done with Big Boy at the Gohannas.

They all liked my attitude, and it was out of their liking for me that I soon became accepted by them—as a mascot, I know now. They would talk about anything and everything with me standing right there hearing them, the same way people would talk freely in front of a pet canary. They would even talk about me, or about "niggers," as though I wasn't there, as if I wouldn't understand what the word meant. A hundred times a day, they used the word "nigger." I suppose that in their own minds, they meant no harm; in fact they probably meant well. It was the same with the cook, Lucille, and her husband, Duane. I remember one day when Mr. Swerlin, as nice as he was, came in from Lansing, where he had been through the Negro section, and said to Mrs. Swerlin right in front of me, "I just can't see how those niggers can be so happy and be so poor." He talked about how they lived in shacks, but had those big, shining cars out front.

And Mrs. Swerlin said, me standing right there, "Niggers are just that way. . . ." That scene always stayed with me.

It was the same with the other white people, most of them local politicians, when they would come visiting the Swerlins. One of their favorite parlor topics was "niggers." One of them was the judge who was in charge of me in Lansing. He was a close friend of the Swerlins. He would ask about me when he came, and they would call me in, and he would look me up and down, his expression approving, like he was examining a fine colt, or a pedigreed pup. I knew they must have told him how I acted and how I worked.

What I am trying to say is that it just never dawned upon them that I could understand, that I wasn't a pet, but a human being. They didn't give me credit for having the same sensitivity, intellect, and understanding that they would have been ready and willing to recognize in a white boy in my position. But it has historically been the case with white people, in their regard for black people, that even though we might be *with* them, we weren't considered *of* them. Even though they appeared to have opened the door, it was still closed. Thus they never did really see *me*.

This is the sort of kindly condescension which I try to clarify today, to these integration-hungry Negroes, about their "liberal" white friends, these so-called "good white people"—most of them anyway. I don't care how nice one is to you; the thing you must always remember is that almost never does he really see you as he sees himself, as he sees his own kind. He may stand with you through thin, but not thick; when the chips are down, you'll find that as fixed in him as his bone structure is his sometimes subconscious conviction that he's better than anybody black.

But I was no more than vaguely aware of anything like that in my detention-home years. I did my little chores around the house, and everything was fine. And each weekend, they didn't mind my catching a ride over to Lansing for the afternoon or evening. If I wasn't old enough, I sure was big enough by then, and nobody ever questioned my hanging out, even at night, in the streets of the Negro section.

I was growing up to be even bigger than Wilfred and Philbert, who had begun to meet girls at the school dances, and other places, and introduced me to a few. But the ones who seemed to like me, I didn't go for—and vice versa. I couldn't dance a lick, anyway, and I couldn't see squandering my few dimes on girls. So mostly I pleasured myself these Saturday nights by gawking around the Negro bars and restaurants. The jukeboxes were wailing Erskine Hawkins' "Tuxedo Junction," Slim and Slam's "Flatfoot Floogie," things like that. Sometimes, big bands from New York, out touring the one-night stands in the sticks, would play for big dances in Lansing. Everybody with legs would come out to see any performer who bore the magic name "New York." Which is how I first heard Lucky Thompson and Milt Jackson, both of whom I later got to know well in Harlem.

Many youngsters from the detention home, when their dates came up, went off to the reform school. But when mine came up—two or three times—it was always ignored. I saw new youngsters arrive and leave. I was glad and grateful. I knew it was Mrs. Swerlin's doing. I didn't want to leave.

She finally told me one day that I was going to be entered in Mason Junior High School. It was the only school in town. No ward of the detention home had ever gone to school there, at least while still a ward. So I entered their seventh grade. The only other Negroes there were some of the Lyons children, younger than I was, in the lower grades. The Lyons and I, as it happened, were the town's only Negroes. They were, as Negroes, very much respected. Mr. Lyons was a smart, hardworking man, and Mrs. Lyons was a very good woman. She and my mother, I had heard my mother say, were two of the four West Indians in that whole section of Michigan.

Some of the white kids at school, I found, were even friendlier than some of those in Lansing had been. Though some, including the teachers, called me "nigger," it was easy to see that they didn't mean any more harm by it than the Swerlins. As the "nigger" of my class, I was in fact extremely popular—I suppose partly because I was kind of a novelty. I was in demand, I had top priority. But I also benefited from the special prestige of having the seal of approval from that Very Important Woman about the town of Mason, Mrs. Swerlin. Nobody in Mason would have dreamed of getting on the wrong side of her. It became hard for me to get through a school day without someone after me to join this or head up that—the debating society, the Junior High basketball team, or some other extracurricular activity. I never turned them down.

And I hadn't been in the school long when Mrs. Swerlin, knowing I could use spending money of my own, got me a job after school washing the dishes in a local restaurant. My boss there was the father of a white classmate whom I spent a lot of time with. His family lived over the restaurant. It was fine working there. Every Friday night when I got paid, I'd feel at least ten feet tall. I forget how much I made, but it seemed like a lot. It was the first time I'd ever had any money to speak of, all my own, in my whole life. As soon as I could afford it, I bought a green suit and some shoes, and at school I'd buy treats for the others in my class—at least as much as any of them did for me.

English and history were the subjects I liked most. My English teacher, I recall—a Mr. Ostrowski—was always giving advice about how to become something in life. The one thing I didn't like about history class was that the teacher, Mr. Williams, was a great one for "nigger" jokes. One day during my first week at school, I walked into the room and he started singing to the class, as a joke, "Way down yonder in the cotton field, some folks say that a nigger won't steal." Very funny. I liked history, but I never thereafter had much liking for Mr. Williams. Later, I remember, we came to the textbook section on Negro history. It was exactly one paragraph long. Mr. Williams laughed through it practically in a single breath, reading aloud how the Negroes had been slaves and then were freed, and how they were usually lazy and dumb and shiftless. He added, I remember, an anthropological footnote on his own, telling us between laughs how Negroes' feet were "so big that when they walk, they don't leave tracks, they leave a hole in the ground."

I'm sorry to say that the subject I most disliked was mathematics. I have thought about it. I think the reason was that mathematics leaves no room for argument. If you made a mistake, that was all there was to it.

Basketball was a big thing in my life, though. I was on the team; we traveled to neighboring towns such as Howell and Charlotte, and wherever I showed my face, the audiences in the gymnasiums "niggered" and "cooned" me to death. Or called me "Rastus." It didn't bother my teammates or my coach at all, and to tell the truth, it bothered me only vaguely. Mine was the same psychology that makes Negroes even today, though it bothers them down inside, keep letting the white man tell them how much "progress" they are making. They've heard it so much they've almost gotten brainwashed into believing it—or at least accepting it.

After the basketball games, there would usually be a school dance. Whenever our team walked into another school's gym for the dance, with me among them, I could feel the freeze. It would start to ease as they saw that I didn't try to mix, but stuck close to someone on our team, or kept to myself. I think I developed ways to do it without making it obvious. Even at our own school, I could sense it almost as a physical barrier, that despite all the beaming and smiling, the mascot wasn't supposed to dance with any of the white girls.

It was some kind of psychic message—not just from them, but also from within myself. I am proud to be able to say that much for myself, at least. I would just stand around and smile and talk and drink punch and eat sandwiches, and then I would make some excuse and get away early.

They were typical small-town school dances. Sometimes a little white band from Lansing would be brought in to play. But most often, the music was a phonograph set up on a table, with the volume turned up high, and the records scratchy, blaring things like Glenn Miller's "Moonlight Serenade"—his band was riding high then—or the Ink Spots, who were also very popular, singing "If I Didn't Care."


In the second semester of the seventh grade, I was elected class president. It surprised me even more than other people. But I can see now why the class might have done it. My grades were among the highest in the school. I was unique in my class, like a pink poodle. And I was proud; I'm not going to say I wasn't. In fact, by then, I didn't really have much feeling about being a Negro, because I was trying so hard, in every way I could, to be white. Which is why I am spending much of my life today telling the American black man that he's wasting his time straining to "integrate." I know from personal experience. I tried hard enough.

"Malcolm, we're just so *proud* of you!" Mrs. Swerlin exclaimed when she heard about my election. It was all over the restaurant where I worked. Even the state man, Maynard Allen, who still dropped by to see me once in a while, had a word of praise. He said he never saw anybody prove better exactly what "reform" meant. I really liked him— except for one thing: he now and then would drop something that hinted my mother had let us down somehow.

Fairly often, I would go and visit the Lyons, and they acted as happy as though I were one of their children. And it was the same warm feeling when I went into Lansing to visit my brothers and sisters, and the Gohannas'.

I remember one thing that marred this time for me: the movie "Gone with the Wind." When it played in Mason, I was the only Negro in the theater, and when Butterfly McQueen went into her act, I felt like crawling under the rug.

Every Saturday, just about, I would go into Lansing. I was going on fourteen, now. Wilfred and Hilda still lived out by themselves at the old family home. Hilda kept the house very clean. It was easier than my mother's plight, with eight of us always under foot or running around. Wilfred worked wherever he could, and he still read every book he could get his hands on. Philbert was getting a reputation as one of the better amateur fighters in this part of the state; everyone really expected that he was going to become a professional.

Reginald and I, after my fighting fiasco, had finally gotten back on good terms. It made me feel great to visit him and Wesley over at Mrs. Williams'. I'd offhandedly give them each a couple of dollars to just stick in their pockets, to have something to spend. And little Yvonne and Robert were doing okay, too, over at the home of the West Indian lady, Mrs. McGuire. I'd give them about a quarter apiece; it made me feel good to see how they were coming along.

None of us talked much about our mother. And we never mentioned our father. I guess none of us knew what to say. We didn't want anybody else to mention our mother either, I think. From time to time, though, we would all go over to Kalamazoo to visit her. Most often we older ones went singly, for it was something you didn't want to have to experience with anyone else present, even your brother or sister.

During this period, the visit to my mother that I most remember was toward the end of that seventh-grade year, when our father's grown daughter by his first marriage, Ella, came from Boston to visit us. Wilfred and Hilda had exchanged some letters with Ella, and I, at Hilda's suggestion, had written to her from the Swerlins'. We were all excited and happy when her letter told us that she was coming to Lansing.

I think the major impact of Ella's arrival, at least upon me, was that she was the first really proud black woman I had ever seen in my life. She was plainly proud of her very dark skin. This was unheard of among Negroes in those days, especially in Lansing.

I hadn't been sure just what day she would come. And then one afternoon I got home from school and there she was. She hugged me, stood me away, looked me up and down. A commanding woman, maybe even bigger than Mrs. Swerlin, Ella wasn't just black, but like our father, she was jet black. The way she sat, moved, talked, did everything, bespoke somebody who did and got exactly what she wanted. This was the woman my father had boasted of so often for having brought so many of their family out of Georgia to Boston. She owned some property, he would say, and she was "in society." She had come North with nothing, and she had worked and saved and had invested in property that she built up in value, and then she started sending money to Georgia for another sister, brother, cousin, niece or nephew to come north to Boston. All that I had heard was reflected in Ella's appearance and bearing. I had never been so impressed with anybody. She was in her second marriage; her first husband had been a doctor.

Ella asked all kinds of questions about how I was doing; she had already heard from Wilfred and Hilda about my election as class president. She asked especially about my grades, and I ran and got my report cards. I was then one of the three highest in the class. Ella praised me. I asked her about her brother, Earl, and her sister, Mary. She had the exciting news that Earl was a singer with a band in Boston. He was singing under the name of Jimmy Carleton. Mary was also doing well.

Ella told me about other relatives from that branch of the family. A number of them I'd never heard of; she had helped them up from Georgia. They, in their turn, had helped up others. "We Littles have to stick together," Ella said. It thrilled me to hear her say that, and even more, the way she said it. I had become a mascot; our branch of the family was split to pieces; I had just about forgotten about being a Little in any family sense. She said that different members of the family were working in good jobs, and some even had small businesses going. Most of them were homeowners.

When Ella suggested that all of us Littles in Lansing accompany her on a visit to our mother, we all were grateful. We all felt that if anyone could do anything that could help our mother, that might help her get well and come back, it would be Ella. Anyway, all of us, for the first time together, went with Ella to Kalamazoo.

Our mother was smiling when they brought her out. She was extremely surprised when she saw Ella. They made a striking contrast, the thin near-white woman and the big black one hugging each other. I don't remember much about the rest of the visit, except that there was a lot of talking, and Ella had everything in hand, and we left with all of us feeling better than we ever had about the circumstances. I know that for the first time, I felt as though I had visited with someone who had some kind of physical illness that had just lingered on.

A few days later, after visiting the homes where each of us were staying, Ella left Lansing and returned to Boston. But before leaving, she told me to write to her regularly. And she had suggested that I might like to spend my summer holiday visiting her in Boston. I jumped at that chance.

That summer of 1940, in Lansing, I caught the Greyhound bus for Boston with my cardboard suitcase, and wearing my green suit. If someone had hung a sign, "HICK," around my neck, I couldn't have looked much more obvious. They didn't have the turnpikes then; the bus stopped at what seemed every corner and cowpatch. From my seat in—you guessed it—the back of the bus, I gawked out of the window at white man's America rolling past for what seemed a month, but must have been only a day and a half.

When we finally arrived, Ella met me at the terminal and took me home. The house was on Waumbeck Street in the Sugar Hill section of Roxbury, the Harlem of Boston. I met Ella's second husband, Frank, who was now a soldier; and her brother Earl, the singer who called himself Jimmy Carleton; and Mary, who was very different from her older sister. It's funny how I seemed to think of Mary as Ella's sister, instead of her being, just as Ella is, my own half-sister. It's probably because Ella and I always were much closer as basic types; we're dominant people, and Mary has always been mild and quiet, almost shy.

Ella was busily involved in dozens of things. She belonged to I don't know how many different clubs; she was a leading light of local so-called "black society." I saw and met a hundred black people there whose big-city talk and ways left my mouth hanging open.

I couldn't have feigned indifference if I had tried to. People talked casually about Chicago, Detroit, New York. I didn't know the world contained as many Negroes as I saw thronging downtown Roxbury at night, especially on Saturdays. Neon lights, nightclubs, poolhalls, bars, the cars they drove! Restaurants made the streets smell—rich, greasy, down-home black cooking! Jukeboxes blared Erskine Hawkins, Duke Ellington, Cootie Williams, dozens of others. If somebody had told me then that some day I'd know them all personally, I'd have found it hard to believe. The biggest bands, like these, played at the Roseland State Ballroom, on Boston's Massachusetts Avenue—one night for Negroes, the next night for whites.

I saw for the first time occasional black-white couples strolling around arm in arm. And on Sundays, when Ella, Mary, or somebody took me to church, I saw churches for black people such as I had never seen. They were many times finer than the white church I had attended back in Mason, Michigan. There, the white people just sat and worshipped with words; but the Boston Negroes, like all other Negroes I had ever seen at church, threw their souls and bodies wholly into worship.

Two or three times, I wrote letters to Wilfred intended for every-body back in Lansing. I said I'd try to describe it when I got back.

But I found I couldn't.

My restlessness with Mason—and for the first time in my life a rest-lessness with being around white people—began as soon as I got back home and entered eighth grade.

I continued to think constantly about all that I had seen in Boston, and about the way I had felt there. I know now that it was the sense of being a real part of a mass of my own kind, for the first time.

The white people—classmates, the Swerlins, the people at the restau-rant where I worked—noticed the change. They said, "You're acting so strange. You don't seem like yourself, Malcolm. What's the matter?"

I kept close to the top of the class, though. The top-most scholastic standing, I remember, kept shifting between me, a girl named Audrey Slaugh, and a boy named Jimmy Cotton.

It went on that way, as I became increasingly restless and disturbed through the first semester. And then one day, just about when those of us who had passed were about to move up to 8-A, from which we would enter high school the next year, something happened which was to become the first major turning point of my life.

Somehow, I happened to be alone in the classroom with Mr. Ostrowski, my English teacher. He was a tall, rather reddish white man and he had a thick mustache. I had gotten some of my best marks under him, and he had always made me feel that he liked me. He was, as I have mentioned, a natural-born "advisor," about what you ought to read, to do, or think—about any and everything. We used to make unkind jokes about him: why was he teaching in Mason instead of somewhere else, getting for himself some of the "success in life" that he kept telling us how to get?

I know that he probably meant well in what he happened to advise me that day. I doubt that he meant any harm. It was just in his nature as an American white man. I was one of his top students, one of the school's top students—but all he could see for me was the kind of future "in your place" that almost all white people see for black people.

He told me, "Malcolm, you ought to be thinking about a career. Have you been giving it thought?"

The truth is, I hadn't. I never have figured out why I told him, "Well, yes, sir, I've been thinking I'd like to be a lawyer." Lansing certainly had no Negro lawyers—or doctors either—in those days, to hold up an image I might have aspired to. All I really knew for certain was that a lawyer didn't wash dishes, as I was doing.

Mr. Ostrowski looked surprised, I remember, and leaned back in his chair and clasped his hands behind his head. He kind of half-smiled and said, "Malcolm, one of life's first needs is for us to be realistic. Don't misunderstand me, now. We all here like you, you know that. But you've got to be realistic about being a nigger. A lawyer —that's no realistic goal for a nigger. You need to think about something you *can* be. You're good with your hands—making things. Everybody admires your carpentry shop work. Why don't you plan on carpentry? People like you as a person—you'd get all kinds of work."

The more I thought afterwards about what he said, the more uneasy it made me. It just kept treading around in my mind.

What made it really begin to disturb me was Mr. Ostrowski's advice to others in my class—all of them white. Most of them had told him they were planning to become farmers. But those who wanted to strike out on their own, to try something new, he had encouraged. Some, mostly girls, wanted to be teachers. A few wanted other professions, such as one boy wanted to become a county agent; another, a veterinarian; and one girl wanted to be a nurse. They all reported that Mr. Ostrowski had encouraged what they had wanted. Yet nearly none of them had earned marks equal to mine.

It was a surprising thing that I had never thought of it that way before, but I realized that whatever I wasn't, I *was* smarter than nearly all of those white kids. But apparently I was still not intelligent enough, in their eyes, to become whatever *I* wanted to be.

It was then that I began to change—inside.

I drew away from white people. I came to class, and I answered when called upon. It became a physical strain simply to sit in Mr. Ostrowski's class.

Where "nigger" had slipped off my back before, wherever I heard it now, I stopped and looked at whoever said it. And they looked surprised that I did.

I quit hearing so much "nigger" and "What's wrong?"—which was the way I wanted it. Nobody, including the teachers, could decide what had come over me. I knew I was being discussed.

In a few more weeks, it was that way, too, at the restaurant where I worked washing dishes, and at the Swerlins'.

One day soon after, Mrs. Swerlin called me into the living room, and there was the state man, Maynard Allen. I knew from their faces that something was about to happen. She told me that none of them could understand why—after I had done so well in school, and on my job, and living with them, and after everyone in Mason had come to like me —I had lately begun to make them all feel that I wasn't happy there anymore.

She said she felt there was no need for me to stay at the detention home any longer, and that arrangements had been made for me to go and live with the Lyons family, who liked me so much.

She stood up and put out her hand. "I guess I've asked you a hundred times, Malcolm—do you want to tell me what's wrong?"

I shook her hand, and said, "Nothing, Mrs. Swerlin." Then I went and got my things, and came back down. At the living room door I saw her wiping her eyes. I felt very bad. I thanked her and went out in front to Mr. Allen, who took me over to the Lyons'.

Mr. and Mrs. Lyons, and their children, during the two months I lived with them—while finishing eighth grade—also tried to get me to tell them what was wrong. But somehow I couldn't tell them, either.

I went every Saturday to see my brothers and sisters in Lansing, and almost every other day I wrote to Ella in Boston. Not saying why, I told Ella that I wanted to come there and live.

I don't know how she did it, but she arranged for official custody of me to be transferred from Michigan to Massachusetts, and the very week I finished the eighth grade, I again boarded the Greyhound bus for Boston.

I've thought about that time a lot since then. No physical move in my life has been more pivotal or profound in its repercussions.

If I had stayed on in Michigan, I would probably have married one of those Negro girls I knew and liked in Lansing. I might have become one of those state capitol building shoeshine boys, or a Lansing Country Club waiter, or gotten one of the other menial jobs which, in those days, among Lansing Negroes, would have been considered "successful"—or even become a carpenter.

Whatever I have done since then, I have driven myself to become a success at it. I've often thought that if Mr. Ostrowski had encouraged me to become a lawyer, I would today probably be among some city's professional black bourgeoisie, sipping cocktails and palming myself off as a community spokesman for and leader of the suffering black masses, while my primary concern would be to grab a few more crumbs from the groaning board of the two-faced whites with whom they're begging to "integrate."

All praise is due to Allah that I went to Boston when I did. If I hadn't, I'd probably still be a brainwashed black Christian.

# BULL FIGHTING A TRAGEDY
## ERNEST HEMINGWAY

It was spring in Paris and everything looked just a little too beautiful. Mike and I decided to go to Spain. Strater drew us a fine map of Spain on the back of a menu of the Strix restaurant. On the same menu he wrote the name of a restaurant in Madrid where the specialty is young suckling pig roasted, the name of a pension on the Via San Jerónimó where the bull fighters live, and sketched a plan showing where the Grecos are hung in the Prado.

Fully equipped with this menu and our old clothes, we started for Spain. We had one objective—to see bull fights.

We left Paris one morning and got off the train at Madrid the next noon. We saw our first bull fight at 4:30 that afternoon. It took about two hours to get tickets. We finally got them from scalpers for twenty-five pesetas apiece. The bull ring was entirely sold out. We had barrera seats. These the scalper explained in Spanish and broken French were the first row of the ringside directly under the royal box, and immediately opposite where the bulls would come out.

We asked him if he didn't have any less distinguished seats for somewhere around twelve pesetas, but he was sold out. So we paid the fifty pesetas for the two tickets, and with the tickets in our pockets sat out on the sidewalk in front of a big café near the Puerta del Sol. It was very exciting, sitting out in front of a café your first day in Spain with a ticket in your pocket that meant that rain or shine you were going to see a bull fight in an hour and a half. In fact, it was so exciting that we started out for the bull ring on the outskirts of the city in about half an hour.

The bull ring or Plaza de Toros was a big, tawny brick amphitheatre standing at the end of a street in an open field. The yellow and red Spanish flag was floating over it. Carriages were driving up and people getting out of buses. There was a great crowd of beggars around the entrance. Men were selling water out of big terra cotta water bottles. Kids sold fans, canes, roasted salted almonds in paper spills, fruit and slabs of ice cream. The crowd was gay and cheerful but all intent on pushing toward the entrance. Mounted civil guards with patent leather cocked hats and carbines slung over their backs sat their horses like statues, and the crowd flowed through.

Inside they all stood around in the bull ring, talking and looking up in the grandstand at the girls in the boxes. Some of the men had field glasses in order to look better. We found our seats and the crowd began to leave the ring and get into the rows of concrete seats. The ring was circular—that sounds foolish, but a boxing ring is square—with a sand floor. Around it was a red board fence—just high enough for a man to be able to vault over it. Between the board fence, which is called the barrera, and the first row of seats ran a narrow alley way. Then came the seats which were just like a football stadium except that around the top ran a double circle of boxes.

Every seat in the amphitheatre was full. The arena was cleared. Then on the far side of the arena out of the crowd, four heralds in medieval costume stood up and blew a blast on their trumpets. The band crashed out, and from the entrance on the far side of the ring four horsemen in black velvet with ruffs around their necks rode out into the white glare of the arena. The people on the sunny side were baking in the heat and fanning themselves. The whole sol side was a flicker of fans.

Behind the four horsemen came the procession of the bull fighters. They had been all formed in ranks in the entrance way ready to march out, and as the music started they came. In the front rank walked the three espadas or toreros, who would have charge of the killing of the six bulls of the afternoon.

They came walking out in heavily brocaded yellow and black costumes, the familiar "toreador" suit, heavy with gold embroidery, cape, jacket, shirt and collar, knee breeches, pink stockings, and low pumps. Always at bull fights afterwards the incongruity of those pink stockings used to strike me. Just behind the three principals—and after your first bull fight you do not look at their costumes but their faces—marched the teams or cuadrillas. They are dressed in the same way but not as gorgeously as the matadors.

Back of the teams ride the picadors. Big, heavy, brown-faced men in wide flat hats, carrying lances like long window poles. They are astride horses that make Spark Plug look as trim and sleek as a King's Plate winner. Back of the pics come the gaily harnessed mule teams and the red-shirted monos or bull ring servants.

The bull fighters march in across the sand to the president's box. They march with easy professional stride, swinging along, not in the least theatrical except for their clothes. They all have the easy grace and slight slouch of the professional athlete. From their faces they might be major league ball players. They salute the president's box and then spread out along the barrera, exchanging their heavy brocaded capes for the fighting capes that have been laid along the red fence by the attendants.

We leaned forward over the barrera. Just below us the three matadors of the afternoon were leaning against the fence talking. One lighted a cigaret. He was a short, clear-skinned gypsy, Gitanillo, in a wonderful gold brocaded jacket, his short pigtail sticking out under his black cocked hat.

"He's not very fancy," a young man in a straw hat, with obviously American shoes, who sat on my left, said.

"But he sure knows bulls, that boy. He's a great killer."

"You're an American, aren't you?" asked Mike.

"Sure," the boy grinned. "But I know this gang. That's Gitanillo. You want to watch him. The kid with the chubby face is Chicuelo. They say he doesn't really like bull fighting, but the town's crazy about him. The next to him is Villalta. He's the great one."

I had noticed Villalta. He was straight as a lance and walked like a young wolf. He was talking and smiling at a friend who leaned over the barrera. Upon his tanned cheekbone was a big patch of gauze held on with adhesive tape.

"He got gored last week at Malaga," said the American.

The American, whom later we were to learn to know and love as the Gin Bottle King, because of a great feat of arms performed at an early hour of the morning with a container of Mr. Gordon's celebrated product as his sole weapon in one of the four most dangerous situations I have ever seen, said: "The show's going to begin."

Out in the arena the picadors had galloped their decrepit horses around the ring, sitting straight and stiff in their rocking chair saddles. Now all but three had ridden out of the ring. These three were huddled against the red painted fence of the barrera. Their horses backed against the fence, one eye bandaged, their lances at rest.

In rode two of the marshals in the velvet jackets and white ruffs. They galloped up to the president's box, swerved and saluted, doffing their hats and bowing low. From the box an object came hurtling down. One of the marshals caught it in his plumed hat.

"The key to the bull pen," said the Gin Bottle King.

The two horsemen whirled and rode across the arena. One of them tossed the key to a man in torero costume, they both saluted with a wave of their plumed hats, and had gone from the ring. The big gate was shut and bolted. There was no more entrance. The ring was complete.

The crowd had been shouting and yelling. Now it was dead silent. The man with the key stepped toward an iron barred, low, red door and unlocked the great sliding bar. He lifted it and stepped back. The door swung open. The man hid behind it. Inside it was dark.

Then, ducking his head as he came up out of the dark pen, a bull came into the arena. He came out all in a rush, big, black and white, weighing over a ton and moving with a soft gallop. Just as he came out the sun seemed to dazzle him for an instant. He stood as though he were frozen, his great crest of muscle up, firmly planted, his eyes looking around, his horns pointed forward, black and white and sharp as porcupine quills. Then he charged. And as he charged I suddenly saw what bull fighting is all about.

For the bull was absolutely unbelievable. He seemed like some great prehistoric animal, absolutely deadly and absolutely vicious. And he was silent. He charged silently and with a soft galloping rush. When he turned he turned on his four feet like a cat. When he charged the first thing that caught his eye was a picador on one of the wretched horses. The picador dug his spurs into the horse and they galloped away. The bull came on in his rush, refused to be shaken off, and in full gallop crashed into the animal from the side, ignored the horse, drove one of his horns high into the thigh of the picador, and tore him, saddle and all, off the horse's back.

The bull went on without pausing to worry the picador lying on the ground. The next picador was sitting on his horse braced to receive the shock of the charge, his lance ready. The bull hit him sideways on, and horse and rider went high up in the air in a kicking mass and fell across the bull's back. As they came down the bull charged into them. The dough-faced kid, Chicuelo, vaulted over the fence, ran toward the bull and flopped his cape into the bull's face. The bull charged the cape and Chicuelo dodged backwards and had the bull clear in the arena.

Without an instant's hesitation the bull charged Chicuelo. The kid stood his ground, simply swung back on his heels and floated his cape like a ballet dancer's skirt into the bull's face as he passed.

"Olé!"—pronounced Oh-Lay!—roared the crowd.


The bull whirled and charged again. Without moving Chicuelo repeated the performance. His legs rigid, just withdrawing his body from the rush of the bull's horns and floating the cape out with that beautiful swing.

Again the crowd roared. The Kid did this seven times. Each time the bull missed him by inches. Each time he gave the bull a free shot at him. Each time the crowd roared. Then he flopped the cape once at the bull at the finish of a pass, swung it around behind him and walked away from the bull to the barrera.

"He's the boy with the cape all right," said the Gin Bottle King. "That swing he did with the cape's called a Veronica."

The chubby faced Kid who did not like bull fighting and had just done the seven wonderful Veronicas was standing against the fence just below us. His face glistened with sweat in the sun but was almost expressionless. His eyes were looking out across the arena where the bull was standing making up his mind to charge a picador. He was studying the bull because a few minutes later it would be his duty to kill him, and once he went out with his thin, red-hilted sword and his piece of red cloth to kill the bull in the final set it would be him or the bull. There are no drawn battles in bull fighting.

I am not going to describe the rest of that afternoon in detail. It was the first bull fight I ever saw, but it was not the best. The best was in the little town of Pamplona high up in the hills of Navarre, and came weeks later. Up in Pamplona, where they have held six days of bull fighting each year since 1126 A.D., and where the bulls race through the streets of the town each morning at six o'clock with half the town running ahead of them. Pamplona, where every man and boy in town is an amateur bull fighter and where there is an amateur fight each morning that is attended by 20,000 people in which the amateur fighters are all unarmed and there is a casualty list at least equal to a Dublin election. But Pamplona, with the best bull fight and the wild tale of the amateur fights, comes in the second chapter.

I am not going to apologize for bull fighting. It is a survival of the days of the Roman Coliseum. But it does need some explanation. Bull fighting is not a sport. It was never supposed to be. It is a tragedy. A very great tragedy. The tragedy is the death of the bull. It is played in three definite acts.

The Gin Bottle King—who, by the way, does not drink gin—told us a lot of this that first night as we sat in the upstairs room of the little restaurant that made a specialty of roast young suckling pig, roasted on an oak plank and served with a mushroom tortilla and vino rojo. The rest we learned later at the bull fighters' pensione in the Via San Jeronimo, where one of the bull fighters had eyes exactly like a rattle-snake.

Much of it we learned in the sixteen fights we saw in different parts of Spain from San Sebastian to Granada.

At any rate bull fighting is not a sport. It is a tragedy, and it sym-bolizes the struggle between man and the beasts. There are usually six bulls to a fight. A fight is called a corrida de toros. Fighting bulls are bred like race horses, some of the oldest breeding establishments being several hundred years old. A good bull is worth about $2,000. They are bred for speed, strength and viciousness. In other words a good fight-ing bull is an absolutely incorrigible bad bull.

Bull fighting is an exceedingly dangerous occupation. In sixteen fights I saw there were only two in which there was no one badly hurt. On the other hand it is very remunerative. A popular espada gets $5,000 for his afternoon's work. An unpopular espada though may not get $500. Both run the same risks. It is a good deal like Grand Opera for the really great matadors except they run the chance of being killed every time they cannot hit high C.

No one at any time in the fight can approach the bull at any time except directly from the front. That is where the danger comes. There are also all sorts of complicated passes that must be done with the cape, each requiring as much technique as a champion billiard player. And underneath it all is the necessity for playing the old tragedy in the absolutely custom bound, law-laid-down way. It must all be done gracefully, seemingly effortlessly and always with dignity. The worst criticism the Spaniards ever make of a bull fighter is that his work is "vulgar."

The three absolute acts of the tragedy are first the entry of the bull when the picadors receive the shock of his attacks and attempt to protect their horses with their lances. Then the horses go out and the second act is the planting of the banderillos. This is one of the most interesting and difficult parts but among the easiest for a new bull fight fan to appreciate in technique. The banderillos are three-foot, gaily colored darts with a small fish hook prong in the end. The man who is going to plant them walks out into the arena alone with the bull. He lifts the banderillos at arm's length and points them toward the bull. Then he calls "Toro! Toro!" The bull charges and the banderillero rises to his toes, bends in a curve forward and just as the bull is about to hit him drops the darts into the bull's hump just back of his horns.

They must go in evenly, one on each side. They must not be shoved, or thrown or stuck in from the side. This is the first time the bull has been completely baffled, there is the prick of the darts that he cannot escape and there are no horses for him to charge into. But he charges the man again and again and each time he gets a pair of the long banderillos that hang from his hump by their tiny barbs and flop like porcupine quills.

Last is the death of the bull, which is in the hands of the matador who has had charge of the bull since his first attack. Each matador has two bulls in the afternoon. The death of the bull is most formal and can only be brought about in one way, directly from the front by the matador who must receive the bull in full charge and kill him with a sword thrust between the shoulders just back of the neck and between the horns. Before killing the bull he must first do a series of passes with the muleta, a piece of red cloth he carries about the size of a large napkin. With the muleta the torero must show his complete mastery of the bull, must make the bull miss him again and again by inches, before he is allowed to kill him. It is in this phase that most of the fatal accidents occur.

The word "toreador" is obsolete Spanish and is never used. The torero is usually called an espada or swordsman. He must be proficient in all three acts of the fight. In the first he uses the cape and does

veronicas and protects the picadors by taking the bull out and away from them when they are spilled to the ground. In the second act he plants the banderillos. In the third act he masters the bull with the muleta and kills him.

Few toreros excel in all three departments. Some, like young Chicuelo, are unapproachable in their cape work. Others like the late Joselito are wonderful banderilleros. Only a few are great killers. Most of the greatest killers are gypsies.

# IN WILDNESS IS THE PRESERVATION OF THE WORLD
## HENRY DAVID THOREAU

**FALL**

Few come to the woods to see how the pine lives and grows and spires, lifting its evergreen arms to the light, to see its perfect success. Most are content to behold it in the shape of many broad boards brought to market, and deem that its true success. The pine is no more lumber than man is, and to be made into boards and houses is no more its true and highest use than the truest use of man is to be cut down and made into manure. A pine cut down, a dead pine, is no more a pine than a dead human carcass is a man. Is it the lumberman who is the friend and lover of the pine, stands nearest to it, and understands its nature best? Is it the tanner or turpentine distiller who posterity will fable was changed into a pine at last? No, no, it is the poet who makes the truest use of the pine, who does not fondle it with an axe, or tickle it with a saw, or stroke it with a plane. It is the poet who loves it as his own shadow in the air, and lets it stand. It is as immortal as I am, and will go to as high a heaven, there to tower above me still. Can he who has only discovered the value of whale-bone and whale-oil be said to have discovered the true uses of the whale? Can he who slays the elephant for his ivory be said to have seen the elephant? No, these are petty and accidental uses. Just as if a stronger race were to kill us in order to make buttons and flageolets of our bones, and then prate of the usefulness of man. Every creature is better alive than dead, both men and moose and pine-trees, as life is more beautiful than death.

It has come to this,—that the lover of art is one, and the lover of nature another, though true art is but the expression of our love of nature. It is monstrous when one cares but little about trees and much about Corinthian columns, and yet this is exceedingly common.

## WINTER

I wish to hear the silence of the night, for the silence is something positive and to be heard. I cannot walk with my ears covered. I must stand still and listen with open ears, far from the noises of the village, that the night may make its impression on me. A fertile and eloquent silence. Sometimes the silence is merely negative, an arid and barren waste in which I shudder, where no ambrosia grows. I must hear the whispering of a myriad voices. Silence alone is worthy to be heard. Silence is of various depths and fertility, like soil. Now it is a mere Sahara, where men perish of hunger and thirst, now a fertile bottom, or prairie, of the West. As I leave the village, drawing nearer to the woods, I listen from time to time to hear the hounds of Silence baying the Moon,—to know if they are on the track of any game. If there's no Diana in the night, what is it worth? . . . The silence rings; it is musical and thrills me. A night in which the silence was audible. I heard the unspeakable.

**SPRING**

When we consider how soon some plants which spread rapidly, by seeds or roots, would cover an area equal to the surface of the globe, . . . how soon some fishes would fill the ocean if all their ova became full-grown fishes, we are tempted to say that every organism, whether animal or vegetable, is contending for the possession of the planet. . . . Nature opposes to this many obstacles, as climate, myriads of brute and also human foes, and of competitors which may preoccupy the ground. Each suggests an immense and wonderful greediness and tenacity of life . . . as if bent on taking entire possession of the globe wherever the climate and soil will permit. And each prevails as much as it does, because of the ample preparations it has made for the contest,—it has secured a myriad chances,—because it never depends on spontaneous generation to save it.

## SUMMER

It is dry, hazy June weather. We are more of the earth, farther from heaven these days. We live in a grosser element. We are getting deeper into the mists of earth. Even the birds sing with less vigor and vivacity. The season of hope and promise is past; already the season of small fruits has arrived. The Indian marked the midsummer as the season when berries were ripe. We are a little saddened, because we begin to see the interval between our hopes and their fulfillment. The prospect of the heavens is taken way, and we are presented only with a few small berries.

There are from time to time mornings, both in summer and in winter, when especially the world seems to begin anew, beyond which memory need not go, for not behind them is yesterday and our past life; when, as in the morning of a hoar frost, there are visible the effects as of a certain creative energy.

... The world has visibly been recreated in the night. Mornings of crea-
tion, I call them. In the midst of these marks of a creative energy recently active, while the sun is rising with more than usual splendor, I look back ... for the era of this creation, not into the night, but to a dawn for which no man ever rose early enough. A morning which carries us back beyond the Mosaic creation, where crystallizations are fresh and unmelted. It is the poet's hour. Mornings when men are new-born, men who have the seeds of life in them.

Every day a new picture is painted and framed, held up for half an hour, in such lights as the Great Artist chooses, and then withdrawn, and the curtain falls. And then the sun goes down, and long the afterglow gives light. And then the damask curtains glow along the western window. And now the first star is lit, and I go home.

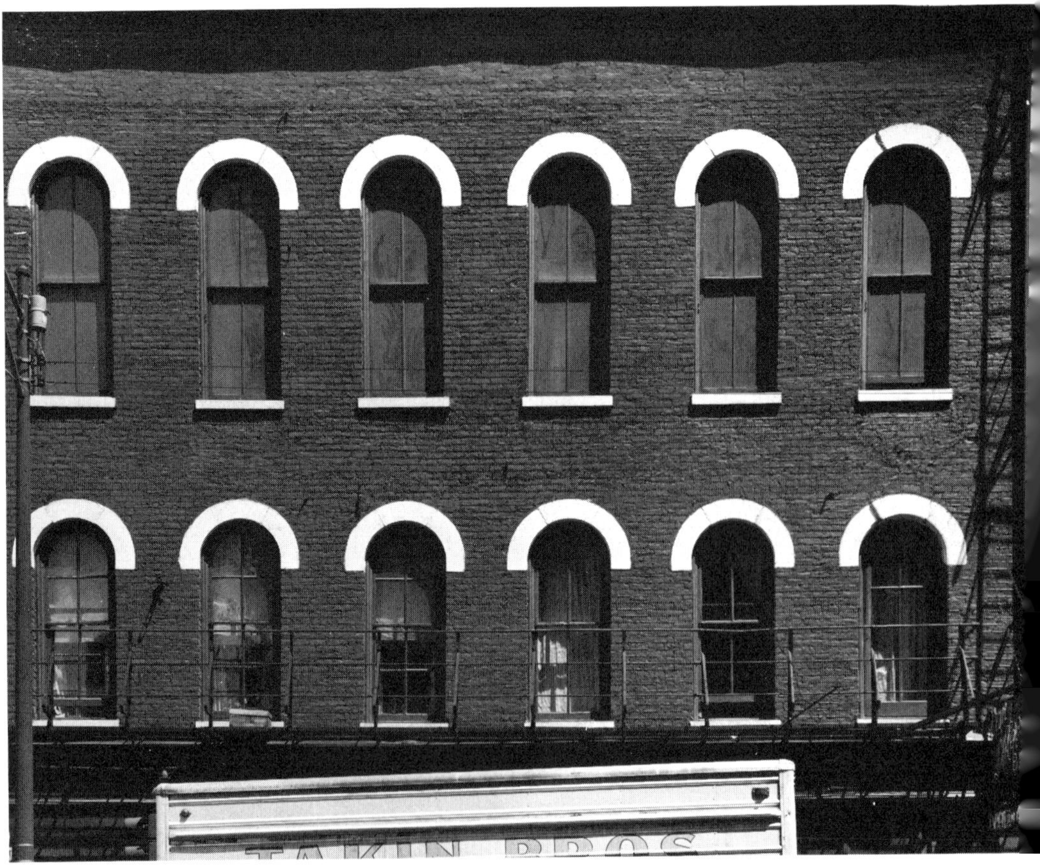

# FROM THE SUBWAY
# TO THE SYNAGOGUE
## ALFRED KAZIN

All my early life lies open to my eye within five city blocks. When I passed the school, I went sick with all my old fear of it. With its standard New York public-school brown brick courtyard shut in on three sides of the square and the pretentious battlements overlooking that cockpit in which I can still smell the fiery sheen of the rubber ball, it looks like a factory over which has been imposed the façade of a castle. It gave me the shivers to stand up in that courtyard again; I felt as if I had been mustered back into the service of those Friday morning "tests" that were the terror of my childhood.

It was never learning I associated with that school: only the necessity to succeed, to get ahead of the others in the daily struggle to "make a good impression" on our teachers, who grimly, wearily, and often with ill-concealed distaste watched against our relapsing into the natural savagery they expected of Brownsville boys. The white, cool, thinly ruled record book sat over us from their desks all day long, and had remorselessly entered into it each day—in blue ink if we had passed, in red ink if we had not—our attendance, our conduct, our "effort," our merits and demerits; and to the last possible decimal point in calculation, our standing in an unending series of "tests"—surprise tests, daily tests, weekly tests, formal midterm tests, final tests. They never stopped trying to dig out of us whatever small morsel of fact we had managed to get down the night before. We had to prove that we were really alert, ready for anything, always in the race. That white thinly ruled record book figured in my mind as the judgment seat; the very thinness and remote blue lightness of its lines instantly showed its cold authority over me; so much space had been left on each page, columns and columns in which to note down everything about us, implacably and forever. As it lay there on a teacher's desk, I stared at it all day long with such fear and anxious propriety that I had no trouble believing that God, too, did nothing but keep such record books, and that on the final day He would face me with an account in Hebrew letters whose phonetic dots and dashes looked strangely like decimal points counting up my every sinful thought on earth.

All teachers were to be respected like gods, and God Himself was the greatest of all school superintendents. Long after I had ceased to believe that our teachers could see with the back of their heads, it was still understood, by me, that they knew everything. They were the delegates of all visible and invisible power on earth—of the mothers who waited on the stoops every day after three for us to bring home tales of our daily triumphs; of the glacially remote Anglo-Saxon principal, whose very name was King; of the incalculably important Superintendent of Schools who would someday rubberstamp his name to the bottom of our diplomas in grim acknowledgment that we had, at last, given satisfaction to him, to the Board of Superintendents, and to our benefactor the City of New York—and so up and up, to the government of the United States and to the great Lord Jehovah Himself. My belief in teachers' unlimited wisdom and power rested not so much on what I saw in them—how impatient most of them looked, how wary—but on our abysmal humility, at least in those of us who were "good" boys, who proved by our ready compliance and "manners" that we wanted to get on. The road to a professional future would be shown us only as we pleased *them. Make a good impression the first day of the term, and they'll help you out. Make a bad impression, and you might as well cut your throat.* This was the first article of school folklore, whispered around the classroom the opening day of each term. You made the "good impression" by sitting firmly at your wooden desk, hands clasped; by silence for the greatest part of the live-long day; by standing up obsequiously when it was so expected of you; by sitting down noiselessly when you had answered a question; by "speaking nicely," which meant reproducing their painfully exact enunciation; by "showing manners," or an ecstatic submissiveness in all things; by outrageous flattery; by bringing little gifts at Christmas, on their birthdays, and at the end of the term—the well-known significance of these gifts being that they came not from us, but from our parents, whose eagerness in this matter showed a high level of social consideration, and thus raised our standing in turn.

It was not just our quickness and memory that were always being tested. Above all, in that word I could never hear without automatically seeing it raised before me in gold-plated letters, it was our *character*. I always felt anxious when I heard the word pronounced. Satisfactory as my "character" was, on the whole, except when I stayed too long in the playground reading; outrageously satisfactory, as I can see now, the very sound of the word as our teachers coldly gave it out from the end of their teeth, with a solemn weight on each dark syllable, immediately struck my heart cold with fear—they could not believe I really had it. Character was never something you had; it had to be trained in you, like a technique. I was never very clear about it. On our side *character* meant demonstrative obedience; but teachers already had it—how else could they have become teachers? They had it; the aloof Anglo-Saxon principal whom we remotely saw only on ceremonial occasions in the assembly was positively encased in it; it glittered off his bald head in spokes of triumphant light; the President of the United States had the greatest conceivable amount of it. Character belonged to great adults. Yet we were constantly being driven onto it; it was the great threshold we had to cross. *Alfred Kazin, having shown proficiency in his course of studies and having displayed satisfactory marks of character . . .* Thus someday the hallowed diploma, passport to my further advancement in high school. But there—I could already feel it in my bones—they would put me through even more doubting tests of character; and after that, if I should be good enough and bright enough, there would be still more. *Character* was a bitter thing, racked with my endless striving to please. The school—from every last stone in the courtyard to the battlements frowning down at me from the walls—was only the stage for a trial. I felt that the very atmosphere of learning that surrounded us was fake—that every lesson, every book, every approving smile was only a pretext for the constant probing and watching of me, that there was not a secret in me that would not be decimally measured into that white record book. All week long I lived for the blessed sound of the dismissal gong at three o'clock on Friday afternoon.

I was awed by this system, I believed in it, I respected its force. The alternative was "going bad." The school was notoriously the toughest in our tough neighborhood, and the dangers of "going bad" were constantly impressed upon me at home and in school in dark whispers of the "reform school" and in examples of boys who had been picked up for petty thievery, rape, or flinging a heavy inkwell straight into a teacher's face. Behind any failure in school yawned the great abyss of a criminal career. Every refractory attitude doomed you with the sound "Sing Sing." Anything less than absolute perfection in school always suggested to my mind that I might fall out of the daily race, be kept back in the working class forever, or—dared I think of it?—fall into the criminal class itself.

I worked on a hairline between triumph and catastrophe. Why the odds should always have felt so narrow I understood only when I realized how little my parents thought of their own lives. It was not for myself alone that I was expected to shine, but for them—to redeem the constant anxiety of their existence. I was the first American child, their offering to the strange new God; I was to be the monument of their liberation from the shame of being—what they were. And that there was shame in this was a fact that everyone seemed to believe as a matter of course. It was in the gleeful discounting of themselves— what do we know?—with which our parents greeted every fresh victory in our savage competition for "high averages," for prizes, for a few condescending words of official praise from the principal at assembly. It was in the sickening invocation of "Americanism"—the word itself accusing us of everything we apparently were not. Our families and teachers seem tacitly agreed that we were somehow to be a little ashamed of what we were. Yet it was always hard to say why this should be so. It was certainly not—in Brownsville!—because we were Jews, or simply because we spoke another language at home, or were absent on our holy days. It was rather that a "refined," "correct," "nice" English was required of us at school that we did not naturally speak, and that our teachers could never be quite sure we would keep. This English was peculiarly the ladder of advancement. Every future young lawyer was known by it. Even the Communists and Socialists on Pitkin Avenue spoke it. It was bright and clean and polished. We were expected to show it off like a new pair of shoes. When the teacher sharply called a question out, then your name, you were expected to leap up, face the class, and eject those new words fluently off the tongue.

There was my secret ordeal: I could never say anything except in the most roundabout way; I was a stammerer. Although I knew all those new words from my private reading—I read walking in the street, to and from the Children's Library on Stone Avenue; on the fire escape and the roof; at every meal when they would let me; read even when I dressed in the morning, propping my book up against the drawers of the bureau as I pulled on my long black stockings—I could never seem to get the easiest words out with the right dispatch, and would often miserably signal from my desk that I did not know the answer rather than get up to stumble and fall and crash on every word. If, angry at always being put down as lazy or stupid, I did get up to speak, the black wooden floor would roll away under my feet, the teacher would frown at me in amazement, and in unbearable loneliness I would hear behind me the groans and laughter: *tuh-tuh-tuh-tuh.*

The word was my agony. The word that for others was so effortless and so neutral, so unburdened, so simple, so exact, I had first to meditate in advance, to see if I could make it, like a plumber fitting together odd lengths and shapes of pipe. I was always preparing words I could speak, storing them away, choosing between them. And often, when the word did come from my mouth in its great and terrible birth, quailing and bleeding as if forced through a thornbush, I would not be able to look the others in the face, and would walk out in the silence, the infinitely echoing silence behind my back, to say it all cleanly back to myself as I walked in the streets. Only when I was alone in the open air, pacing the roof with pebbles in my mouth, as I had read Demosthenes had done to cure himself of stammering; or in the street, where all words seemed to flow from the length of my stride and the color of the houses as I remembered the perfect tranquillity of a phrase in Beethoven's *Romance in F* I could sing back to myself as I walked—only then was it possible for me to speak without the infinite premeditations and strangled silences I toiled through whenever I got up at school to respond with the expected, the exact answer.

It troubled me that I could speak in the fullness of my own voice only when I was alone on the streets, walking about. There was something unnatural about it; unbearably isolated. I was not like the others! I was not like the others! At midday, every freshly shocking Monday noon, they sent me away to a speech clinic in a school in East New York, where I sat in a circle of lispers and cleft palates and foreign accents holding a mirror before my lips and rolling difficult sounds over and over. To be sent there in the full light of the opening week, when everyone else was at school or going about his business, made me feel as if I had been expelled from the great normal body of humanity. I would gobble down my lunch on my way to the speech clinic and rush back to the school in time to make up for the classes I had lost. One day, one unforgettable dread day, I stopped to catch my breath on a corner of Sutter Avenue, near the wholesale fruit markets, where an old drugstore rose up over a great flight of steps. In the window were dusty urns of colored water floating off iron chains; cardboard placards advertising hairnets, Ex-Lax; a great illustrated medical chart headed THE HUMAN FACTORY, which showed the exact course a mouthful of food follows as it falls from chamber to chamber of the body. I hadn't meant to stop there at all, only to catch my breath; but I so hated the speech clinic that I thought I would delay my arrival for a few minutes by eating my lunch on the steps. When I took the sandwich out of my bag, two bitterly hard pieces of hard salami slipped out of my hand and fell through a grate onto a hill of dust below the steps. I remember how sickeningly vivid an odd thread of hair looked on the salami, as if my lunch were turning stiff with death. The factory whistles called their short, sharp blasts stark through the middle of noon, beating at me where I sat outside the city's magnetic circle. I had never known, I knew instantly I would never in my heart again submit to, such wild passive despair as I felt at that moment, sitting on the steps before THE HUMAN FACTORY, where little robots gathered and shoveled the food from chamber to chamber of the body. They had put me out into the streets, I thought to myself; with their mirrors and their everlasting pulling at me to imitate their effortless bright speech and their stupefaction that a boy could stammer and stumble on every other English word he carried in his head, they had put me out into the streets, had left me high and dry on the steps of that drugstore staring at the remains of my lunch turning black and grimy in the dust.

# THE DOG THAT BIT PEOPLE
## JAMES THURBER

Probably no one man should have as many dogs in his life as I have had, but there was more pleasure than distress in them for me except in the case of an Airedale named Muggs. He gave me more trouble than all the other fifty-four or -five put together, although my moment of keenest embarrassment was the time a Scotch terrier named Jeannie, who had just had six puppies in the clothes closet of a fourth floor apartment in New York, had the unexpected seventh and last at the corner of Eleventh Street and Fifth Avenue during a walk she had insisted on taking. Then, too, there was the prize winning French poodle, a great big black poodle—none of your little, untroublesome white miniatures—who got sick riding in the rumble seat of a car with me on her way to the Greenwich Dog Show. She had a red rubber bib tucked around her throat and, since a rain storm came up when we were half way through the Bronx, I had to hold over her a small green umbrella, really more of a parasol. The rain beat down fearfully and suddenly the driver of the car drove into a big garage, filled with mechanics. It happened so quickly that I forgot to put the umbrella down and I will always remember, with sickening distress, the look of incredulity mixed with hatred that came over the face of the particular hardened garage man who came over to see what we wanted, when he took a look at me and the poodle. All garage men, and people of that intolerant stripe, hate poodles with their curious haircut, especially the pom-poms that you got to leave on their hips if you expect the dogs to win a prize.

But the Airedale, as I have said, was the worst of all my dogs. He really wasn't my dog, as a matter of fact: I came home from a vacation one summer to find that my brother Roy had bought him while I was away. A big, burly, choleric dog, he always acted as if he thought I wasn't one of the family. There was a slight advantage in being one of the family, for he didn't bite the family as often as he bit strangers. Still, in the years that we had him he bit everybody but mother, and he made a pass at her once but missed. That was during the month when we suddenly had mice, and Muggs refused to do anything about them.

Nobody ever had mice exactly like the mice we had that month. They acted like pet mice, almost like mice somebody had trained. They were so friendly that one night when mother entertained at dinner the Frira-liras, a club she and my father had belonged to for twenty years, she put down a lot of little dishes with food in them on the pantry floor so that the mice would be satisfied with that and wouldn't come into the dining room. Muggs stayed out in the pantry with the mice, lying on the floor, growling to himself—not at the mice, but about all the people in the next room that he would have liked to get at. Mother slipped out into the pantry once to see how everything was going. Everything was going fine. It made her so mad to see Muggs lying there, oblivious of the mice—they came running up to her—that she slapped him and he slashed at her, but didn't make it. He was sorry immediately, mother said. He was always sorry, she said, after he bit someone, but we could not understand how she figured this out. He didn't act sorry.

Mother used to send a box of candy every Christmas to the people the Airedale bit. The list finally contained forty or more names. Nobody could understand why we didn't get rid of the dog. I didn't understand it very well myself, but we didn't get rid of him. I think that one or two people tried to poison Muggs—he acted poisoned once in a while—and old Major Moberly fired at him once with his service revolver near the Seneca Hotel in East Broad Street—but Muggs lived to be almost eleven years old and even when he could hardly get around he bit a Congressman who had called to see my father on business. My mother had never liked the Congressman—she said the signs of his horoscope showed he couldn't be trusted (he was Saturn with the moon in Virgo)—but she sent him a box of candy that Christmas. He sent it right back, probably because he suspected it was trick candy. Mother persuaded herself it was all for the best that the dog had bitten him, even though father lost an important business association because of it. "I wouldn't be associated with such a man," mother said. "Muggs could read him like a book."

We used to take turns feeding Muggs to be on his good side, but that didn't always work. He was never in a very good humor, even after a meal. Nobody knew exactly what was the matter with him, but whatever it was it made him irascible, especially in the mornings. Roy never felt very well in the morning, either, especially before breakfast, and once when he came downstairs and found that Muggs had moodily chewed up the morning paper he hit him in the face with a grapefruit and then jumped up on the dining room table, scattering dishes and silverware and spilling the coffee. Muggs' first free leap carried him all the way across the table and into a brass fire screen in front of the gas grate but he was back on his feet in a moment and in the end he got Roy and gave him a pretty vicious bite in the leg. Then he was all over it; he never bit anyone more than once at a time. Mother always mentioned that as an argument in his favor; she said he had a quick temper but that he didn't hold a grudge. She was forever defending him. I think she liked him because he wasn't well. "He's not strong," she would say, pityingly, but that was inaccurate; he may not have been well but he was terribly strong.

One time my mother went to the Chittenden Hotel to call on a woman mental healer who was lecturing in Columbus on the subject of "Harmonious Vibrations." She wanted to find out if it was possible to get harmonious vibrations into a dog. "He's a large tan-colored Airedale," mother explained. The woman said that she had never treated a dog but she advised my mother to hold the thought that he did not bite and would not bite. Mother was holding the thought the very next morning when Muggs got the iceman but she blamed that slip-up on the iceman. "If you didn't think he would bite you, he wouldn't," mother told him. He stomped out of the house in a terrible jangle of vibrations.

One morning when Muggs bit me slightly, more or less in passing, I reached down and grabbed his short stumpy tail and hoisted him into the air. It was a foolhardy thing to do and the last time I saw my mother, about six months ago, she said she didn't know what possessed me. I don't either, except that I was pretty mad. As long as I held the dog off the floor by his tail he couldn't get at me, but he twisted and jerked so, snarling all the time, that I realized I couldn't hold him that way very long. I carried him to the kitchen and flung him onto the floor and shut the door on him just as he crashed against it. But I forgot about the backstairs. Muggs went up the backstairs and down the frontstairs and had me cornered in the living room. I managed to get up onto the mantelpiece above the fireplace, but it gave way and came down with a tremendous crash throwing a large marble clock, several vases, and myself heavily to the floor. Muggs was so alarmed by the racket that when I picked myself up he had disappeared. We couldn't find him anywhere, although we whistled and shouted, until old Mrs. Detweiler called after dinner that night. Muggs had bitten her once, in the leg, and she came into the living room only after we assured her that Muggs had run away. She had just seated herself when, with a great growling and scratching of claws, Muggs emerged from under a davenport where he had been quietly hiding all the time, and bit her again. Mother examined the bite and put arnica on it and told Mrs. Detweiler that it was only a bruise. "He just bumped you," she said. But Mrs. Detweiler left the house in a nasty state of mind.

Lots of people reported our Airedale to the police but my father held a municipal office at the time and was on friendly terms with the police. Even so, the cops had been out a couple times—once when Muggs bit Mrs. Rufus Sturtevant and again when he bit Lieutenant-Governor Malloy—but mother told them that it hadn't been Muggs' fault but the fault of the people who were bitten. "When he starts for them, they scream," she explained, "and that excites him." The cops suggested that it might be a good idea to tie the dog up, but mother said that it mortified him to be tied up and that he wouldn't eat when he was tied up.

Muggs at his meals was an unusual sight. Because of the fact that if you reached toward the floor he would bite you, we usually put his food plate on top of an old kitchen table with a bench alongside the table. Muggs would stand on the bench and eat. I remember that my mother's Uncle Horatio, who boasted that he was the third man up Missionary Ridge, was splutteringly indignant when he found out that we fed the dog on a table because we were afraid to put his plate on the floor. He said he wasn't afraid of any dog that ever lived and that he would put the dog's plate on the floor if we give it to him. Roy said that if Uncle Horatio had fed Muggs on the ground just before the battle he would have been the first man up Missionary Ridge. Uncle Horatio was furious. "Bring him in! Bring him in now!" he shouted. "I'll feed the —— on the floor!" Roy was all for giving him a chance, but my father wouldn't hear of it. He said that Muggs had already been fed. "I'll feed him again!" bawled Uncle Horatio. We had quite a time quieting him.

In his last year Muggs used to spend practically all of his time outdoors. He didn't like to stay in the house for some reason or other—perhaps it held too many unpleasant memories for him. Anyway, it was hard to get him to come in and as a result the garbage man, the iceman, and the laundryman wouldn't come near the house. We had to haul the garbage down to the corner, take the laundry out and bring it back, and meet the iceman a block from home. After this had gone on for some time we hit on an ingenious arrangement for getting the dog in the house so that we could lock him up while the gas meter was read, and so on. Muggs was afraid of only one thing, an electrical storm. Thunder and lightning frightened him out of his senses (I think he thought a storm had broken the day the mantelpiece fell). He would rush into the house and hide under a bed or in a clothes closet. So we fixed up a thunder machine out of a long narrow piece of sheet iron with a wooden handle on one end. Mother would shake this vigorously when she wanted to get Muggs into the house. It made an excellent imitation of thunder, but I suppose it was the most roundabout system for running a household that was ever devised. It took a lot out of mother.

A few months before Muggs died, he got to "seeing things." He would rise slowly from the floor, growling low, and stalk stiff-legged and menacing toward nothing at all. Sometimes the Thing would be just a little to the right or left of a visitor. Once a Fuller Brush salesman got hysterics. Muggs came wandering into the room like Hamlet following his father's ghost. His eyes were fixed on a spot just to the left of the Fuller Brush man, who stood it until Muggs was about three slow, creeping paces from him. Then he shouted. Muggs wavered on past him into the hallway grumbling to himself but the Fuller man went on shouting. I think mother had to throw a pan of cold water on him before he stopped. That was the way she used to stop us boys when we got into fights.

Muggs died quite suddenly one night. Mother wanted to bury him in the family lot under a marble stone with some such inscription as "Flights of angels sing thee to thy rest" but we persuaded her it was against the law. In the end we just put up a smooth board above his grave along a lonely road. On the board I wrote with an indelible pencil "Cave Canem." Mother was quite pleased with the simple classic dignity of the old Latin epitaph.

# MY DUNGEON SHOOK:
# LETTER TO MY NEPHEW
## JAMES BALDWIN


Dear James:

I have begun this letter five times and torn it up five times. I keep seeing your face, which is also the face of your father and my brother. Like
him, you are tough, dark, vulnerable, moody—with a very definite tendency to sound truculent because you want no one to think you are
soft. You may be like your grandfather in this, I don't know, but certainly both you and your father resemble him very much physically.
Well, he is dead, he never saw you, and he had a terrible life; he was
defeated long before he died because, at the bottom of his heart, he
really believed what white people said about him. This is one of the
reasons that he became so holy. I am sure that your father has told you
something about all that. Neither you nor your father exhibit any tendency towards holiness: you really *are* of another era, part of what
happened when the Negro left the land and came into what the late
E. Franklin Frazier called "the cities of destruction." You can only be
destroyed by believing that you really are what the white world calls a
*nigger*. I tell you this because I love you, and please don't you forget it.

I have known both of you all your lives, have carried your Daddy in
my arms and on my shoulders, kissed and spanked him and watched
him learn to walk. I don't know if you've known anybody from that far
back; if you've loved anybody that long, first as an infant, then as a
child, then as a man, you gain a strange perspective on time and human
pain and effort. Other people cannot see what I see whenever I look
into your father's face, for behind your father's face as it is today are all
those other faces which were his. Let him laugh and I see a cellar your
father does not remember and a house he does not remember and I
hear in his present laughter his laughter as a child. Let him curse and I
remember him falling down the cellar steps, and howling, and I remember, with pain, his tears, which my hand or your grandmother's
so easily wiped away. But no one's hand can wipe away those tears he
sheds invisibly today, which one hears in his laughter and in his speech

and in his songs. I know what the world has done to my brother and how narrowly he has survived it. And I know, which is much worse, and this is the crime of which I accuse my country and my countrymen, and for which neither I nor time nor history will ever forgive them, that they have destroyed and are destroying hundreds of thousands of lives and do not know it and do not want to know it. One can be, indeed one must strive to become, tough and philosophical concerning destruction and death, for this is what most of mankind has been best at since we have heard of man. (But remember: *most* of mankind is not *all* of mankind.) But it is not permissible that the authors of devastation should also be innocent. It is the innocence which constitutes the crime.

Now, my dear namesake, these innocent and well-meaning people, your countrymen, have caused you to be born under conditions not very far removed from those described for us by Charles Dickens in the London of more than a hundred years ago. (I hear the chorus of the innocents screaming, "No! This is not true! How *bitter* you are!"—but I am writing this letter to *you*, to try to tell you something about how to handle *them*, for most of them do not yet really know that you exist. I *know* the conditions under which you were born, for I was there. Your countrymen were *not* there, and haven't made it yet. Your grandmother was also there, and no one has ever accused her of being bitter. I suggest that the innocents check with her. She isn't hard to find. Your countrymen don't know that *she* exists, either, though she has been working for them all their lives.)

Well, you were born, here you came, something like fourteen years ago; and though your father and mother and grandmother, looking about the streets through which they were carrying you, staring at the walls into which they brought you, had every reason to be heavy-hearted, yet they were not. For here you were, Big James, named for me—you were a big baby, I was not—here you were: to be loved. To be loved, baby, hard, at once, and forever, to strengthen you against the loveless world. Remember that: I know how black it looks today, for you. It looked bad that day, too, yes, we were trembling. We have not stopped trembling yet, but if we had not loved each other none of us would have survived. And now you must survive because we love you, and for the sake of your children and your children's children.

This innocent country set you down in a ghetto in which, in fact, it intended that you should perish. Let me spell out precisely what I mean by that, for the heart of the matter is here, and the root of my dispute with my country. You were born where you were born and faced the future that you faced because you were black and *for no other reason*. The limits of your ambition were, thus, expected to be set forever. You were born into a society which spelled out with brutal clarity, and in as many ways as possible, that you were a worthless human being. You were not expected to aspire to excellence: you were expected to make peace with mediocrity. Wherever you have turned, James, in your short time on this earth, you have been told where you could go and what you could do (and *how* you could do it) and where you could live and whom you could marry. I know your countrymen do not agree with me about this, and I hear them saying, "You exaggerate." They do not know Harlem, and I do. So do you. Take no one's word for anything, including mine—but trust your experience. Know whence you came. If you know whence you came, there is really no limit to where you can go. The details and symbols of your life have been deliberately constructed to make you believe what white people say about you. Please try to remember that what they believe, as well as what they do and cause you to endure, does not testify to your inferiority but to their inhumanity and fear. Please try to be clear, dear James, through the storm which rages about your youthful head today, about the reality which lies behind the words *acceptance* and *integration*. There is no reason for you to try to become like white people and there is no basis whatever for their impertinent assumption that *they* must accept *you*. The really terrible thing, old buddy, is that *you* must accept *them*. And I mean that very seriously. You must accept them and accept them with love. For these innocent people have no other hope. They are, in effect, still trapped in a history which they do not understand; and until they understand it, they cannot be released from it. They have had to believe for many years, and for innumerable reasons, that black men are inferior to white men. Many of them, indeed, know better, but, as you will discover, people find it very difficult to act on what they know. To act is to be committed, and to be committed is to be in danger. In this case, the danger, in the minds of most white Americans, is the loss of their identity. Try to imagine how you would feel if you woke up one morning to find the sun shining and all the stars aflame. You would be frightened because it is out of the order of nature. Any upheaval in the universe is terrifying because it so profoundly attacks one's sense of one's own reality. Well, the black man has functioned in the white man's world as a fixed star, as an immovable pillar: and as he moves out of his place, heaven and earth are shaken to their foundations. You, don't be afraid. I said that it was intended that you should perish in the ghetto, perish by never being allowed to go behind the white man's definitions, by never being allowed to spell your proper name. You have, and many of us have, defeated this intention; and, by a terrible law, a terrible paradox, those innocents who believed that your imprisonment made them safe are losing their grasp of reality. But these men are your brothers—your lost, younger brothers. And if the word *integration* means anything, this is what it means: that we, with love, shall force our brothers to see themselves as they are, to cease fleeing from reality and begin to change it. For this is your home, my friend, do not be driven from it; great men have done great things here, and will again, and we can make America what America must become. It will be hard, James, but you come from sturdy, peasant stock, men who picked cotton and dammed rivers and built railroads, and, in the teeth of the most terrifying odds, achieved an unassailable and monumental dignity. You come from a long line of great poets, some of the greatest poets since Homer. One of them said, *The very time I thought I was lost, My dungeon shook and my chains fell off.*

You know, and I know, that the country is celebrating one hundred years of freedom one hundred years too soon. We cannot be free until they are free. God bless you, James, and Godspeed.

Your uncle,
James

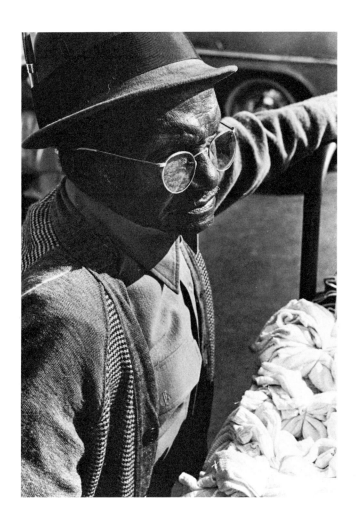

# WORD PLAY

GARGLE  *ATTEN*TION

DETONATE  RABBIT

STOWAWAY

detache d  maGNify

milli,ooo,ooonaire

NEWTN

TEDDY RSEVELT

PICASS

SEGOVIA

J. EDGAR HOOVER

# MORALS AND WEAPONS
## KONRAD LORENZ

It is early one Sunday morning at the beginning of March, when Easter is already in the air, and we are taking a walk in the Vienna forest whose wooded slopes of tall beeches can be equalled in beauty by few and surpassed by none. We approach a forest glade. The tall, smooth trunks of the beeches soon give place to the Hornbeam, which are clothed from top to bottom with pale green foliage. We now tread slowly and more carefully. Before we break through the last bushes and out of cover on to the free expanse of the meadow, we do what all wild animals and all good naturalists, wild boars, leopards, hunters and zoologists would do under similar circumstances: we reconnoitre, seeking, before we leave our cover, to gain from it the advantage which it can offer alike to hunter and hunted, namely, to see without being seen.

Here, too, this age-old strategy proves beneficial. We do actually see someone who is not yet aware of our presence, as the wind is blowing away from him in our direction. In the middle of the clearing sits a large, fat hare. He is sitting with his back to us, making a big V with his ears, and is watching intently something on the opposite edge of the meadow. From this point, a second and equally large hare emerges and with slow, dignified hops, makes his way towards the first one. There follows a measured encounter, not unlike the meeting of two strange dogs. This cautious, mutual taking stock soon develops into sparring. The two hares chase each other round, head to tail, in minute circles. This giddy rotating continues for quite a long time. Then suddenly, their pent-up energies burst forth into a battle royal. It is just like the outbreak of war, and happens at the very moment when the long mutual threatening of the hostile parties has forced one to the conclusion that neither dares to make a definite move. Facing each other, the hares rear up on their hind legs and, straining to their full height, drum furiously at each other with their fore pads. Now they clash in flying leaps and, at last, to the accompaniment of squeals and grunts, they discharge a volley of lightning kicks, so rapidly that only a slow motion camera could help us to discern the mechanism of these hostilities. Now, for the time being, they have had enough, and they recommence their circling, this time much faster than before; then follows a fresh, more embittered bout. So engrossed are the two champions, that there is nothing to prevent me and my little daughter from tiptoeing nearer, although that venture cannot be accomplished in silence. Any normal and sensible hare would have heard us long ago, but this is March, and March Hares are mad! The whole boxing match looks so comical that my little daughter, in spite of her iron upbringing in the matter of silence when watching animals, cannot restrain a chuckle. That is too much even for March Hares—two flashes in two different directions and the meadow is empty, while over the battlefield floats a fistful of fluff, light as a thistledown.

It is not only funny, it is almost touching, this duel of the unarmed, this raging fury of the meek in heart. But are these creatures really so meek? Have they really got softer hearts than those of the fierce beasts of prey? If, in a zoo, you ever watched two lions, wolves or eagles in conflict, then, in all probability, you did not feel like laughing. And yet, these sovereigns come off no worse than the harmless hares. Most people have the habit of judging carnivorous and herbivorous animals by quite inapplicable moral criteria. Even in fairy tales, animals are portrayed as being a community comparable to that of mankind, as though all species of animals were beings of one and the same family, as human beings are. For this reason, the average person tends to regard the animal that kills animals in the same light as he would the man that kills his own kind. He does not judge the fox that kills a hare by the same standard as the hunter who shoots one for precisely the same reason, but with that severe censure that he would apply to the gamekeeper who made a practice of shooting farmers and frying them for supper! The "wicked" beast of prey is branded as a murderer, although the fox's hunting is quite as legitimate and a great deal more necessary to his existence than is that of the gamekeeper, yet nobody regards the latter's "bag" as his prey, and only one author, whose own standards were indicted by the severest moral criticism, has dared to dub the fox-hunter "the unspeakable in pursuit of the uneatable"! In their dealing with members of their own species, the beasts and birds of prey are far more restrained than many of the "harmless" vegetarians.

Still more harmless than a battle of hares appears the fight between turtle- or ring-doves. The gentle pecking of the frail bill, the light flick of the fragile wing seems, to the uninitiated, more like a caress than an attack. Some time ago I decided to breed a cross between the African blond ring-dove and our own indigenous somewhat frailer turtle-dove, and, with this object, I put a tame, home-reared male turtle-dove and a female ring-dove together in a roomy cage. I did not take their original scrapping seriously. How could these paragons of love and virtue dream of harming one another? I left them in their cage and went to Vienna. When I returned, the next day, a horrible sight met my eyes. The turtle-dove lay on the floor of the cage; the top of his head and neck, as also the whole length of his back, were not only plucked bare of feathers, but so flayed as to form a single wound dripping with blood. In the middle of this gory surface, like an eagle on his prey, stood the second harbinger of peace. Wearing that dreamy facial expression that so appeals to our sentimental observer, this charming lady pecked mercilessly with her silver bill in the wounds of her prostrated mate. When the latter gathered his last resources in a final effort to escape, she set on him again, struck him to the floor with a light clap of her wing and continued with her slow pitiless work of destruction. Without my interference she would undoubtedly have finished him off, in spite of the fact that she was already so tired that she could hardly keep her eyes open. Only in two other instances have I seen similar horrible lacerations inflicted on their own kind by vertebrates: once, as an observer of the embittered fights of cichlid fishes who sometimes actually skin each other, and again as a field surgeon, in the late war, where the highest of all vertebrates prepetrated mass mutilations on members of his own species. But to return to our "harmless" vegetarians. The battle of the hares which we witnessed in the forest clearing would have ended in quite as horrible a carnage as that of the doves, had it taken place in the confines of a cage where the vanquished could not flee the victor.

If this is the extent of the injuries meted out to their own kind by our gentle doves and hares, how much greater must be the havoc wrought amongst themselves by those beasts to whom nature has relegated the strongest weapons with which to kill their prey? One would certainly think so, were it not that a good naturalist should always check by observation even the most obvious-seeming inferences before he accepts them as truth. Let us examine that symbol of cruelty and voraciousness, the wolf. How do these creatures conduct themselves in their dealings with members of their own species? At Whipsnade, that zoological country paradise, there lives a pack of timber wolves. From the fence of a pine-wood of enviable dimensions we can watch their daily round in an environment not so very far removed from conditions of real freedom. To begin with, we wonder why the antics of the many woolly, fat-pawed whelps have not led them to destruction long ago. The efforts of one ungainly little chap to break into a gallop have landed him in a very different situation from that which he inteded. He stumbles and bumps heavily into a wicked-looking old sinner. Strangely enough, the latter does not seem to notice it, he does not even growl. But now we hear the rumble of battle sounds! They are low, but more ominous than those of a dog-fight. We were watching the whelps and have therefore only become aware of this adult fight now that it is already in full swing.

An enormous old timber wolf and a rather weaker, obviously younger one are the opposing champions and they are moving in circles round each other, exhibiting admirable "footwork." At the same time, the bared fangs flash in such a rapid exchange of snaps that the eye can scarcely follow them. So far, nothing has really happened. The jaws of one wolf close on the gleaming white teeth of the other, who is on the alert and wards off the attack. Only the lips have received one or two minor injuries. The younger wolf is gradually being forced backwards. It dawns upon us that the older one is purposely maneuvering him towards the fence. We wait with breathless anticipation what will happen when he "goes to the wall." Now he strikes the wire netting, stumbles . . . and the old one is upon him. And now the incredible happens, just the opposite of what you would expect. The furious whirling of the grey bodies has come to a sudden standstill. Shoulder to shoulder they stand, pressed against each other in a stiff and strained attitude, both heads now facing in the same direction. Both wolves are growling angrily, the elder in a deep bass, the younger in higher tones, suggestive of the fear that underlies his threat. But notice carefully the position of the two opponents; the older wolf has his muzzle close, very close against the neck of the younger, and the latter holds away his head, offering up-protected to his enemy the bend of his neck, the most vulnerable part of his whole body! Less than an inch from the tensed neck-muscles, where the jugular vein lies immediately beneath the skin, gleam the fangs of his antagonist from beneath the wickedly retracted lips. Whereas, during the thick of the fight, both wolves were intent on keeping only their teeth, the one invulnerable part of the body, in opposition to each other, it now appears that the discomfited fighter proffers intentionally that part of his anatomy to which a bite must assuredly prove fatal. Appearances are notoriously deceptive, but in his case, surprisingly, they are not!

This same scene can be watched any time wherever street-mongrels are to be found. I cited wolves as my first example because they illustrate my point more impressively than the all too familiar domestic dog. Two adult male dogs meet in the street. Stiff-legged, with tails erect and hair on end, they pace towards each other. The nearer they approach, the stiffer, higher and more ruffled they appear, their advance becomes slower and slower. Unlike fighting cocks they do not make their encounter head to head, front against front, but make as though to pass each other, only stopping when they stand at last flank to flank, head to tail, in close juxtaposition. Then a strict ceremonial demands that each should sniff the hind regions of the other. Should one of the dogs be overcome with fear at this juncture, down goes his tail between his legs and he jumps with a quick, flexible twist, wheeling at an angle of 180 degrees thus modestly retracting his former offer to be smelt. Should the two dogs remain in an attitude of self display, carrying their tails as rigid as standards, then the sniffing process may be of a long, protracted nature. All may be solved amicably, and there is still the chance that first one tail and then the other may begin to wag with small but rapidly increasing beats and then this nerve-racking situation may develop into nothing worse than a cheerful canine romp. Failing this solution the situation becomes more and more tense, noses begin to wrinkle and to turn up with a vile, brutal expression, lips begin to curl, exposing the fangs on the side nearer the opponent. Then the animals scratch the earth angrily with their hind feet, deep growls rise from their chests, and, in the next moment, they fall upon each other with loud piercing yells.

But to return to our wolves, whom we left in a situation of acute tension. This was not a piece of inartistic narrative on my part, since the strained situation may continue for a great length of time which is minutes to the observer, but very probably seems hours to the losing wolf. Every second you expect violence and await with bated breath the moment when the winner's teeth will rip the jugular vein of the loser. But your fears are groundless, for it will not happen. In this particular situation, the victor will definitely not close on his less fortunate rival. You can see that he would like to, but he just cannot! A dog or wolf that offers its neck to its adversary in this way will never be bitten seriously. The other growls and grumbles, snaps with his teeth in the empty air and even carries out, without delivering so much as a bite, the movement of shaking something to death in the empty air. However, this strange inhibition from biting persists only so long as the defeated dog or wolf maintains his attitude of humility. Since the fight is stopped so suddenly by this action, the victor frequently finds himself straddling his vanquished foe in anything but a comfortable position. So to remain, with his muzzle applied to the neck of the "underdog," soon becomes tedious for the champion, and, seeing that he cannot bite anyway, he soon withdraws. Upon this, the under-dog may hastily attempt to put distance between himself and his superior. But he is not usually successful in this, for, as soon as he abandons his rigid attitude of submission, the other again falls upon him like a thunderbolt and the victim must again freeze into his former posture. It seems as if the victor is only waiting for the moment when the other will relinquish his submissive attitude, thereby enabling him to give vent to his urgent desire to bite. But, luckily for the "under-dog," the top-dog at the close of the fight is overcome by the pressing need to leave his trade-mark on the battlefield, to designate it as his personal property— in other words, he must lift his leg against the nearest upright object. This right-of-possession ceremony is usually taken advantage of by the underdog to make himself scarce.

By this commonplace observation, we are here, as so often, made conscious of a problem which is actual in our daily life and which confronts us on all sides in the most various forms. Social inhibitions of this kind are not rare, but so frequent that we take them for granted and do not stop to think about them. An old German proverb says that one crow will not peck out the eye of another, and for once the proverb is right. A tame crow or raven will no more think of pecking at your eye than he will at that of one of his own kind. Often when Roah, my tame raven, was sitting on my arm, I purposely put my face so near to his bill that my open eye came close to its wickedly curved point. Then Roah did something positively touching. With a nervous, worried movement he withdrew his beak from my eye, just as a father who is shaving will hold back his razor blade from the inquisitive fingers of his tiny daughter. Only in one particular connection did Roah ever approach my eye with his bill during this facial grooming. Many of the higher, social birds and mammals, above all monkeys, will groom the skin of a fellow-member of their species in those parts of his body to which he himself cannot obtain access. In birds, it is particularly the head and the region of the eyes which are dependent on the attentions of a fellow. In my description of the jackdaw, I have already spoken of the gestures with which these birds invite one another to preen their head feathers. When, with half-shut eyes, I held my head sideways towards Roah, just as corvine birds do to each other, he understood this movement in spite of the fact that I have no head feathers to ruffle, and at once began to groom me. While doing so, he never pinched my skin, for the epidermis of birds is delicate and would not stand such rough treatment. With wonderful precision, he submitted every attainable hair to a dry-cleaning process by drawing it separately through his bill. He worked with the same intensive concentration that distinguishes the "lousing" monkey and the operating surgeon. This is not meant as a joke: the social grooming of monkeys, and particularly of anthropoid apes has not the object of catching vermin— these animals usually have none—and is not limited to the cleaning of the skin, but serves also more remarkable operations, for instance the dexterous removal of thorns and even the squeezing-out of small carbuncles.

The manipulations of the dangerous-looking corvine beak round the open eye of a man naturally appear ominous and, of course, I was always receiving warnings from onlookers at this procedure. "You never know—a raven is a raven—" and similar words of wisdom. I used to respond with the paradoxical observation that the warner was for me potentially more dangerous than the raven. It has often happened that people have been shot dead by madmen who have masked their condition with the cunning and pretense typical of such cases. There was always a possibility, though admittedly a very small one, that our kind adviser might be afflicted with such a disease. But a sudden and unpredictable loss of the eye-pecking inhibition in a healthy, mature raven is more unlikely by far than an attack by a well-meaning friend.

Why has the dog the inhibition against biting his fellow's neck? Why has the raven an inhibition against pecking the eye of his friend? Why has the ring-dove no such "insurance" against murder? A really comprehensive answer to these questions is almost impossible. It would certainly involve a *historical* explanation of the process by which these inhibitions have been developed in the course of evolution. There is no doubt that they have arisen side by side with the development of the dangerous weapons of the beast of prey. However, it is perfectly obvious why these inhibitions are necessary to all weapon-bearing animals. Should the raven peck, without compunction, at the eye of his nest-mate, his wife or his young, in the same way as he pecks at any other moving and glittering object, there would, by now, be no more ravens in the world. Should a dog or wolf unrestrainedly and unaccountably bite the neck of his pack-mates and actually execute the movement of shaking them to death, then his species also would certainly be exterminated within a short space of time.

The ring-dove does not require such an inhibition since it can only inflict injury to a much lesser degree, while its ability to flee is so well developed that it suffices to protect the bird even against enemies equipped with vastly better weapons. Only under the unnatural conditions of close confinement which deprive the losing dove of the possibility of flight does it become apparent that the ring-dove has no inhibitions which prevent it from injuring or even torturing its own kind. Many other "harmless" herbivores prove themselves just as unscrupulous when they are kept in narrow captivity. One of the most disgusting, ruthless and blood-thirsty murderers is an animal which is generally considered as being second only to the dove in the proverbial gentleness of its nature, namely the roe-deer. The roe-buck is about the most malevolent beast I know and is possessed, into the bargain, of a weapon, its antlers, which it shows mighty little restraint in putting into use. The species can "afford" this lack of control since the fleeing capacity even of the weakest doe is enough to deliver it from the strongest buck.

Only in very large paddocks can the roe-buck be kept with females of his own kind. In smaller enclosures, sooner or later he will drive his fellows, females and young ones included, into a corner and gore them to death. The only "insurance against murder" which the roe-deer possesses is based on the fact that the onslaught of the attacking buck proceeds relatively slowly. He does not rush with lowered head at his adversary as, for example, a ram would do, but he approaches quite slowly, cautiously feeling with his antlers for those of his opponent. Only when the antlers are interlocked and the buck feels firm resistance does he thrust with deadly earnest. According to the statistics given by W. T. Hornaday, the former director of the New York Zoo, tame deer cause yearly more serious accidents than captive lions and tigers, chiefly because an uninitiated person does not recognize the slow approach of the buck as an earnest attack, even when the animal's antlers have come dangerously near. Suddenly there follows, thrust upon thrust, the amazingly strong stabbing movement of the sharp weapon, and you will be lucky if you have time enough to get a good grip on the aggressor's antlers. Now there follows a wrestling match in which the sweat pours and the hands drip blood, and in which even a very strong man can hardly obtain mastery over the roe-buck unless he succeeds in getting to the side of the beast and bending his neck backwards. Of course, one is ashamed to call for help—until one has the point of an antler in one's body! So take my advice and if a charming, tame roe-buck comes playfully toward you, with a characteristic prancing step and flourishing his antlers gracefully, hit him, with your walking stick, a stone or the bare fist, as hard as you can, on the side of his nose, before he can apply his antlers to your person.

And now, honestly judged: who is really a "good" animal, my friend Roah to whose social inhibitions I could trust the light of my eyes, or the gentle ring-dove that in hours of hard work nearly succeeded in torturing its mate to death? Who is a "wicked" animal, the roe-buck who will slit the bellies even of females and young of his own kind if they are unable to escape him, or the wolf who cannot bite his hated enemy if the latter appeals to his mercy?

Now let us turn our mind to another question. Wherein consists the essence of all the gestures of submission by which a bird or animal of a social species can appeal to the inhibitions of its superior? We have just seen, in the wolf, that the defeated animal actually facilitates his own destruction by offering to the victor those very parts of his body which he was most anxious to shield as long as the battle was raging. All submissive attitudes with which we are so far familiar, in social animals, are based on the same principle: The supplicant always offers to his adversary the most vulnerable part of his body, or, to be more exact, that part *against which every killing attack is inevitably directed!* In most birds, this area is the base of the skull. If one jackdaw wants to show submission to another, he squats back on his hocks, turns away his head, at the same time drawing in his bill to make the nape of his neck bulge, and, leaning towards his superior, seems to invite him to peck at the fatal spot. Seagulls and herons present to their superior the top of their head, stretching their neck forward horizontally, low over the ground, also a position which makes the supplicant particularly defenceless.

With many gallinaceous birds, the fights of the males commonly end by one of the combatants being thrown to the ground, held down and then scalped as in the manner described in the ring-dove. Only one species shows mercy in this case, namely the turkey: and this one only does so in response to a specific submissive gesture which serves to forestall the intent of the attack. If a turkey-cock has had more than his share of the wild and grotesque wrestling match in which these birds indulge, he lays himself with outstretched neck upon the ground. Whereupon the victor behaves exactly as a wolf or dog in the same situation, that is to say, he evidently *wants* to peck and kick at the prostrated enemy, but simply cannot: he would if he could but he can't! So, still in threatening attitude, he walks round and round his prostrated rival, making tentative passes at him, but leaving him untouched.

This reaction—though certainly propitious for the turkey species—can cause a tragedy if a turkey comes to blows with a peacock, a thing which not infrequently happens in captivity, since these species are closely enough related to "appreciate" respectively their mutual manifestations of virility. In spite of greater strength and weight the turkey nearly always loses the match, for the peacock flies better and has a different fighting technique. While the red-brown American is muscling himself up for the wrestling match, the blue East-Indian has already flown above him and struck at him with his sharply pointed spurs. The turkey justifiably considers this infringement of his fighting code as unfair and, although he is still in possession of his full strength, he throws in the sponge and lays himself down in the above depicted manner now. And a ghastly thing happens: the peacock does not "understand" this submissive gesture of the turkey, that is to say, it elicits no inhibition of his fighting drives. He pecks and kicks further at the helpless turkey, who, if nobody comes to his rescue, is doomed, for the more pecks and blows he receives, the more certainly are his escape reactions blocked by the submissive attitude. It does not and cannot occur to him to jump up and run away.

The fact that many birds have developed special "signal organs" for eliciting this type of social inhibition, shows convincingly the blind instinctive nature and the great evolutionary age of these submissive gestures. The young of the water-rail, for example, have a bare red patch at the back of their head which, as they present it meaningly to an older and stronger fellow, takes on a deep red color. Whether, in higher animals and man, social inhibitions of this kind are equally mechanical, need not for the moment enter into our consideration. Whatever may be the reasons that prevent the dominant individual from injuring the submissive one is immaterial to the practical issue. The essential behavior of the submissive as well as of the dominant partner remains the same: the humbled creature suddenly seems to lose his objections to being injured and removes all obstacles from the path of the killer, and it would seem that the very removal of these outer obstacles raises an insurmountable inner obstruction in the central nervous system of the aggressor.

And what is a human appeal for mercy after all? Is it so very different from what we have just described? The Homeric warrior who wishes to yield and plead mercy, discards helmet and shield, falls on his knees and inclines his head, a set of actions which should make it easier for the enemy to kill, but, in reality, hinders him from doing so. As Shakespeare makes Nestor say of Hector:

> Thou hast hung thy advanced sword i' the air,
> Not letting it decline on the declined.

Even today, we have retained many symbols of such submissive attitudes in a number of our gestures of courtesy: bowing, removal of the hat, and presenting arms in military ceremonial. If we are to believe the ancient epics, an appeal to mercy does not seem to have raised an "inner obstruction" which was entirely insurmountable. Homer's heroes were certainly not as soft-hearted as the wolves of Whipsnade! In any case, the poet cites numerous instances where the supplicant was slaughtered with or without compunction. The Norse heroic sagas bring us many examples of similar failures of the submissive gesture and it was not till the era of knight-errantry that it was no longer considered "sporting" to kill a man who begged for mercy. The Christian knight is the first who, for reasons of traditional and religious morals, is as chivalrous as is the wolf from the depth of his natural impulses and inhibitions. What a strange paradox!

The worker in comparative ethology does well to be very careful in applying moral criteria to animal behavior. But here, I must myself own to harboring sentimental feelings: I think it a truly magnificent thing that one wolf finds himself unable to bite the proffered neck of the

other, but still more so that the other relies upon him for this amazing restraint. I, at least, have extracted from it a new and deeper understanding of a wonderful and often misunderstood saying from the Gospel which hitherto had only awakened in me feeling of strong opposition "And unto him that smiteth thee on the one cheek offer also the other." (St. Luke vi 26). A wolf has enlightened me: not so that your enemy may strike you again do you turn the other cheek toward him, but to make him unable to do it.

When, in the course of its evolution, a species of animals develops a weapon which may destroy a fellow-member at one blow, then, in order to survive, it must develop, along with the weapon, a social inhibition to prevent a usage which could endanger the existence of the species. Among the predatory animals, there are only a few which lead so solitary a life that they can, in general, forego such restraint. They come together only at the mating season when the sexual impulse outweighs all others, including that of aggression. Such unsociable hermits

are the polar bear and the jaguar and, owing to the absence of these social inhibitions, animals of these species, when kept together in Zoos, hold a sorry record for murdering their own kind. The system of special inherited impulses and inhibitions, together with the weapons with which a social species is provided by nature, form a complex which is carefully computed and self-regulating. All living beings have received their weapons through the same process of evolution that molded their impulses and inhibitions, for the structural plan of the body and the system of behavior of a species are part of the same whole.

> If such be Nature's holy plan,
> Have I not reason to lament
> What man has made of man?

Wordsworth is right: there is only one being in possession of weapons which do not grow on his body and of whose working plan, therefore, the instincts of his species know nothing and in the usage of which he has no correspondingly adequate inhibition. That being is man. With unarrested growth, his weapons increase in monstrousness, multiplying horribly within a few decades. But innate impulses and inhibitions, like bodily structures, need time for their development, time on a scale in which geologists and astronomers are accustomed to calculate, and not historians. We did not receive our weapons from nature. We made them ourselves, of our own free will. Which is going to be easier for us in the future, the production of the weapons or the engendering of the feeling of responsibility that should go along with them, the inhibitions without which our race must perish by virtue of its own creations? We must build up these inhibitions purposefully for we cannot rely upon our instincts. Fourteen years ago, I concluded an article on "Morals and Weapons of Animals" which appeared in a Viennese journal, with the words, "The day will come when two warring factions will be faced with the possibility of each wiping the other out completely. The day may come when the whole of mankind is divided into two such opposing camps. Shall we then behave like doves or like wolves? The fate of mankind will be settled by the answer to this question." We may well be apprehensive.

# WAR

## WAR PRAYER

O Lord our Father, our young patriots, idols of our hearts, go forth to battle—be thou near them! With them—in spirit—we also go forth from the sweet peace of our beloved firesides to smite the foe. O Lord, Our God, help us tear their soldiers to bloody shreds with our shells; help us to cover their smiling fields with the pale forms of their patriot dead; help us to drown the thunder of their guns with the shrieks of their wounded, writhing in pain; help us to lay waste their humble homes with a hurricane of fire; help us to wring the hearts of their unoffending widows with unavailing grief; help us to turn them out roofless with their little children to wander unfriended the wastes of the desolated land in rags and hunger and thirst . . .

**MARK TWAIN**

# A GLIMPSE OF WAR'S HELL-SCENES

In one of the late movements of our troops in the valley (near Upperville, I think), a strong force of Moseby's mounted guerrillas attacked a train of wounded and the guard of cavalry convoying them. The ambulances contained about sixty wounded, quite a number of them officers of rank. The rebels were in strength, and the capture of the train and its partial guard after a short snap was effectually accomplished. No sooner had our men surrendered, the rebels instantly commenced robbing the train and murdering their prisoners, even the wounded. Here is the scene or a sample of it, ten minutes after. Among the wounded officers in the ambulances were one, a lieutenant of regulars, and another of higher rank. These two were dragged out on the ground on their backs, and were now surrounded by the guerrillas, a demoniac crowd, each member of which was stabbing them in different parts of their bodies. One of the officers had his feet pinned firmly to the ground by bayonets stuck through them and thrust into the ground. These two officers, as afterward found on examination, had received about twenty such thrusts, some of them through the mouth, face, etc. The wounded had all been dragged (to give a better chance also for plunder) out of their wagons; some had been effectually dispatched, and their bodies were lying there lifeless and bloody. Others, not yet dead, but horribly mutilated, were moaning or groaning. Of our men who surrendered, most had been thus maimed or slaughtered.

At this instant a force of our cavalry, who had been following the train at some interval, charged suddenly upon the secesh captors, who proceeded at once to make the best escape they could. Most of them got away, but we gobbled two officers and seventeen men, in the very acts just described. The sight was one which admitted of little discussion, as may be imagined. The seventeen captured men and two officers were put under guard for the night, but it was decided there and then that they should die. The next morning the two officers were taken in the town, separate places, put in the center of the street, and shot. The seventeen men were taken to an open ground, a little one side. They were placed in a hollow square, half-encompassed by two of our cavalry regiments, one of which regiments had three days before found the bloody corpses of three of their men hamstrung and hung up by the heels to limbs of trees by Moseby's guerrillas, and the other had not long before had twelve men, after surrendering, shot and then hung by the neck to limbs of trees, and jeering inscriptions pinned to the breast of one of the corpses, who had been a sergeant. Those three, and those twelve, had been found, I say, by these environing regiments. Now, with revolvers, they formed the grim cordon of the seventeen prisoners. The latter were placed in the midst of the hollow square, unfastened, and the ironical remark made to them that they were now to be given "a chance for themselves." A few ran for it. But what use? From every side the deadly pills came. In a few minutes the seventeen corpses strewed the hollow square. I was curious to know whether some of the Union soldiers, some few (some one or two at least of the youngsters), did not abstain from shooting on the helpless men. Not one. There was no exultation, very little said, almost nothing, yet every man there contributed his shot.

Multiply the above by scores, aye hundreds—verify it in all the forms that different circumstances, individuals, places, could afford—light it with every lurid passion, the wolf's, the lion's lapping thirst for blood —the passionate, boiling volcanoes of human revenge for comrades, brothers slain—with the light of burning farms, and heaps of smutting, smoldering black embers—and in the human heart everywhere black, worse embers—and you have an inkling of this war.

**WALT WHITMAN**

# VIGIL STRANGE I KEPT ON THE FIELD ONE NIGHT

Vigil strange I kept on the field one night;
When you my son and my comrade dropt at my side that day,
One look I but gave which your dear eyes return'd with a look
    I shall never forget,
One touch of your hand to mine O boy, reach'd up as you lay
    on the ground,
Then onward I sped in the battle, the even-contested battle,
Till late in the night reliev'd to the place at last again
    I made my way,
Found you in death so cold dear comrade, found your body
    son of responding kisses, (never again on earth responding,)
Bared your face in the starlight, curious the scene, cool blew
    the moderate night-wind,
Long there and then in vigil I stood, dimly around me the
    battlefield spreading,
Vigil wondrous and vigil sweet there in the fragrant
    silent night,
But not a tear fell, not even a long-drawn sigh, long, long
    I gazed,
Then on the earth partially reclining sat by your side leaning
    my chin in my hands,
Passing sweet hours, immortal and mystic hours with you
    dearest comrade—not a tear, not a word,

Vigil of silence, love and death, vigil for you my son and
    my soldier,
As onward silently stars aloft, eastward new ones upward stole,
Vigil final for you brave boy, (I could not save you, swift
    was your death,
I faithfully loved you and cared for you living, I think we
    shall surely meet again,)
Till at latest lingering of the night, indeed just as the dawn
    appear'd,
My comrade I wrapt in his blanket, envelop'd well his form,
Folded the blanket well, tucking it carefully over head and
    carefully under feet,
And there and then and bathed by the rising sun, my son in his
    grave, in his rude-dug grave I deposited,
Ending my vigil strange with that, vigil of night and battle-
    field dim,
Vigil for boy of responding kisses, (never again on earth
    responding,)
Vigil for comrade swiftly slain, vigil I never forget, how as
    day brighten'd,
I rose from the chill ground and folded my soldier well in
    his blanket,
And buried him where he fell.

**WALT WHITMAN**

# TIME IS SHORT
# AND THE WATER RISES
## JOHN WALSH, with ROBERT GANNON

*Operation Gwamba began when ISPA (the International Society for the Protection of Animals) learned that thousands of forest creatures were trapped by the spreading artificial lake behind the new Afobaka Dam in Surinam—formerly Dutch Guiana. To Surinam, ISPA sent John Walsh, a young man trained in rescue techniques by the Massachusetts SPCA. What followed was one of this century's most extraordinary true adventures of man and animal—the story of the rescue of 10,000 animals from certain death in a South American rain forest.*

When my tranquilizer guns—three rifles and a pistol—arrived in customs shortly after the project started, they posed a problem for the Surinam authorities: How were they to be classified? Were they really guns? Were they "traps," as are nets? Or would the classification fall under "medical equipment," because of the syringes, needles, and drugs?

Customs officials, typical of the genre, settled the problem by moving the equipment to a side room, hoping that we would forget about it. Official explanation for the delay was "We're working on it; just a couple more days," and it stood that way for weeks. Finally I threw the problem in Commissioner Michel's lap. Then, because a commissioner's authority is virtually boundless, the guns were released in only another three weeks.

Ten years ago hardly anyone had heard of tranquilizer guns. Newly introduced at that time and barely understood, they were used mainly to pacify zoo animals. A shot of the drug Sparine would tranquilize a tiger, for instance, so he could be examined without the vet fearing loss of an arm. The tiger wouldn't be out, just tranquil. Soon zookeepers and others began employing larger charges and stronger drugs to knock out the animals, and today tranquilizer guns are widely used by humane groups, dogcatchers, zoologists, ranchers, and conservationists. (Actually, they're "immobilizer guns," but nobody calls them that but the manufacturer.)

Essentially, a tranquilizer rifle works this way: Two small cylinders of compressed carbon dioxide—the same as used in air pistols—are snapped under the barrel, and gas pressure builds up behind the projectile, basically an aluminum hypodermic needle. The gun goes off with a "pffft" instead of a bang. The rifle is accurate to thirty-five yards or so, the pistol to only about ten.

When the syringe hits, the needle penetrates the skin, and a plunger drives forward to inject the knockout substance—primarily a nicotine alkaloid. Early models used a mixture of acetic acid and sodium bicarbonate or carbide and water to shove the plunger forward. The shock of firing would jar the chemical loose from little containers and mix them, causing bubbling. By the time the projectile hit, the effervescence would have started slowly to slide the plunger, to inject the charge under the skin.

There were two troubles, though. Sometimes the bubbling worked so well all the drug had squirted out en route. Other times, when the animal was struck, it wouldn't stand still long enough. A monkey, for instance, would reach back, pull out the missile, and trot off not even sleepy. Today syringes are activated explosively. When the projectile hits, an internal spring-loaded 22-caliber power charge fires, driving the plunger forward and injecting the knockout substance in a fraction of a second.

Some weeks earlier I had told the men I had a gun in Boston that puts animals to sleep. They all laughed and joked and thought it was a good story. When the equipment was released, I told nobody about it other than Robb, and only he knew what I had in mind when we set off for an island some twenty miles south of the dam. It had been underwater for a few weeks now. Before it submerged, we had swept it clean of all terrestrial animals, then after many of the leaves had died and fallen, we removed most of the arboreal creatures. The only species left that we knew about was the red howler monkey, a monkey huge by South American standards (including the tail, it's more than a yard long), and his name comes from his most impressive voice.

The island of Gran Pati (meaning "big split") always had been an island. The Surinam River split around it, isolating a piece of land five miles long, two wide. Water now had killed most of the trees, and was submerging even the tops of those originally growing at the island's periphery. Actually, though, the time was somewhat early to go after red howlers. There was too much room left for them to move in, and miripa seeds—howler food—were still plentiful. But I was anxious to try out the gun, to see if it was at all practical for jungle use.

We paddled, pushed, and pulled the boats through the trees for a while, then high above us, maybe seventy-five feet, we saw the troupe, ten or fifteen howlers chattering and watching us and swinging through the branches. I opened the tranquilizer gun case. "This is the gun that puts animals to sleep," I dramatically announced to the men. "I'll shoot the king, and in a few minutes he'll fall asleep." They were laughing now. Even Robb asked me under his breath if I were sure it would work.

A red howler troupe always has a king, a leader. I picked him out, waited until he was in the clear, and shot. Earlier I had set up the gun with the howler in mind, carefully measuring my guess of the correct dose (about 1½ cubic centimeters), preparing three syringes, just in case I missed.

I did. The missile streaked upward, pinged off a branch, and was never seen again. I reloaded and shot, sensing that shooting in a rain forest is not as easy as in a Massachusetts field. This one hit the limb under the monkey, stuck fast, and, squeezing knockout solution forward, strove to put the branch to sleep.

Then the third projectile. Success; it hit the monk smack in the left rear leg and stuck there. He stopped short, turned around and looked at it, pulled it out, and threw it down into the water. Then he went skipping off through the trees again.

The Bushnegroes laughed and hooted and rocked back and forth in the boats and shouted at each other. They thought the monkey had showed me up. But I motioned to Sime to stay with the king, because I knew the syringe had injected a big enough dose.

Soon the king halted, out on the end of a branch about thirty feet up. He began to rock back and forth, and the men went "woo-ooo-ooo-ooo" and stopped laughing. The monkey swayed, tried to hold his balance, then slowly slid around to the underside of the branch. He let go with his arms and legs, and like a pendulum swung gently to and fro, hanging by his tail. I hopped to the back of the boat, grabbed one of the long-handled nets, and held it under the branch. "Now he's going to fall," I said—and sure enough, he did, right into the net. What a production.

"Oh, you killed him, boss," said Sime, and I was a little surprised to hear that his voice was pensive.

I rolled my subject out on the dugout bottom and looked at his furriness. His long, thick coat, predominantly dark red, looked actually metallic close up, with glowing shimmers of gold, copper, and bronze. The top of his tail was heavily furred, but its underside was bald—the better to grip branches with. "Tonight when it gets dark, he'll be waking up," I announced.

On our way back to camp, we passed an island that once had been two miles across, but by now had shrunk to just a spot. We'd covered it twice already, once to capture the larger ground-living animals—deer, mostly—then later, when it had dwindled to a hundred yards across, to scoop up the smaller beasts: agoutis, pacas, armadillos.

I signaled Sime to turn the boat and to idle down so we barely moved. We picked our way first through the treetops at the outer edge, then through the trunks as the water became shallower, then through the newly submerged ferns, still green—but a brownish green—as they fountained from the water. Ahead was the only remaining spot of solid land—a hilltop now six feet across. If anything at all is left, I thought, it will be here.

I expected to see turtles, perhaps, or rats, or maybe snakes. What we did find were toads, scores of them—some in the water, bobbing in the waves made by our boat, the rest squeezed onto the little plot of ground, two, three deep. These were the giant *Bufo marinus,* called neotropical toads, common throughout northern South America and Central America, occasionally seen in Mexico and even Texas. But nowhere do these, the largest tailless amphibians in the world, grow as large as in the Guianas. Most of these had a diameter of maybe six inches, but a few were as large as LP records, ten, twelve inches—larger than any I had ever read about. The biggest ones all were females, and each had a male rider clinging piggyback, his forefeet grabbing little fingerholds handily located just back of her ears, waiting for her to just try to lay eggs without his participation.

We stepped overboard into the shallow water and started scooping the dozens of flaccid amphibians into the boat. Most were extremely skinny, sluggish, and weak from lack of food, but when I tried to pull a male from the back of his beloved, his foreleg muscles seemed to be made of steel.

The whole bottom of the boat was a warty, hopping mass a half foot deep when we set out again. The drugged howler monkey, fortunately, remained unconscious. He'd be unhappy if he came to. He was half submerged in toads.

Along the lakeside, on the way back to camp, we stopped four times to scoop out the giant toads, who, like great mounds of animated lichen, went plopping off into the forest.

It was after we returned to camp that I began worrying about the monkey. He should be waking now, I figured, but instead he was comatose, dangerously so, I felt. His heart was barely pumping, his breathing, shallow and plodding, was slowing even more. I must have given him an overdose.

Then his breathing stopped altogether, and his gums and tongue began to turn blue from lack of oxygen. I pulled the sprawling 25-pound body onto my lap and began squeezing his upper chest rhythmically, wondering how fast a monkey's respiration rate is supposed to be. I squeezed and squeezed and soon he began breathing again. Then he stopped, turned blue, and I squeezed again. The sequence continued, and finally I settled myself in a chair with the monkey on my lap and a book propped up in front of me and spent the next two and a half hours squeezing until he began breathing, then letting him go on his own until he stopped, then squeezing again. My hands got tired, then numb, as the ache worked its way up my arms into my shoulders. Finally the periods during which the monkey breathed by himself lengthened. The respiration became regular, the heart strong, and finally I could relax. Now every once in a while his eyelids fluttered.

I left him lying there, sprawled out on the box in the middle of camp. Every so often the men gathered around him would feel his beating heart or watch his eyes twitch, reassuring themselves that he actually was still alive. Then around seven o'clock he began to raise his head, look around and drop again, and each time he did his audience would exclaim and comment and laugh. Soon he sat up, and we slid him into a cage (we planned to hold him at camp until we captured the rest of his troupe, then release them all together), and he contented himself by spending the rest of the evening scowling at whoever looked his way.

The men called the tranquilizer rifle *doemi goeni*—sleep gun—and word of its magic quickly spread up the river. Throughout my stay, whenever I'd go into a strange village, the captain casually would mention that he had heard the story—undoubtedly a fabrication—that I had a *doemie goeni*, some device that would put animals to sleep. I'd verify that it was so, but I could tell he still didn't quite believe it, not unless one of my men was with me, another Bushnegro that the captain could really trust.

In many situations the guns were a blessing, but we quickly learned that they were no panacea. Shooting a hypodermic syringe through a rain-forest canopy is extremely difficult. Any little leaf or twig in the flight path will cause it to miss the target, and deflected needles rarely can be found. They're expensive, too; each needle costs from two to five dollars, depending on size. And maintenance was a problem. The guns were always being thrown hurriedly into the bottom of the boat as we took off after animals, there to be stepped upon or flooded with water.

The biggest problem, though, was deciding how much drug each kind of animal should get. We had two choices of the nicotine solution: One was fast-acting with a narrow margin of safety, a bigger chance of overdosing and killing the animal. The other was slow-acting, and if an overdose were accidentally given, the animal simply would sleep longer. Usually, when shooting a new kind of animal, we'd guess the amount needed, then use the slow-acting, high-safety solution a few times. When we were sure of the amount, we'd switch to the other concentration.

The slow-acting material was less desirable, mainly because being struck with an exploding hypodermic syringe panics many animals, and if the drug acts too slowly, the animal might escape, only to become dazed and collapse later, vulnerable to predators.

Our general yardstick was based on North American animals, a certain ratio of solution to body weight (cubic centimeters per pound), depending on species and solution concentration. But the trouble was, things didn't work out in nice, parallel steps. A tapir might weigh four times as much as a man, but will need ten times as much drug to achieve the same effect. Large, hoofed animals—North American cattle and deer, for instance—require about one cubic centimeter per one hundred pounds. But if you use that ratio on small animals, like foxes or raccoons, they are hardly fazed. You have to step up the ratio to one cubic centimeter per twenty-five pounds—a fourfold relative increase.

We never did find what some animals require. The giant armadillo, for instance. Giant armadillos are relatively rare in Surinam, or at least in the area we worked, for in the whole eighteen months of the project we caught only seven of them in the 650-square-mile area. We tranquilized our first *Priodontes giganteus* on an island a mile long and half mile wide, a former hilltop ten miles upriver from the dam.

The morning was half gone when Robb and I arrived. Bally, Deo, and the dogs were hollering and crashing through the brush, herding whatever was on the island to men waiting in the boats. We paddled up just as the dogs began to bark frantically, a somewhat different kind of bark than I had heard before.

We beached and ran toward the sound, as usual crashing through the foliage like madmen, stickers and thorns and vines bouncing off us. Then we broke into a sort of clearing, and stopped. Still. Like something out of a Tertiary fantasy, the giant armadillo stood swaying and slowly turning its hundred-pound massiveness. Its shell was a yard long; add another yard for its bony snout and its scaly tail. Three dogs were facing it, yelping their fool heads off, while the animal stood at bay. One of the dogs dashed for the armadillo's tail. The quarry spun with astonishing speed, whipping his forefoot around toward the dog. He missed, and it's good he did. An armadillo's middle finger on the forefoot is equipped with a four-inch claw, sickle-shaped and vicious. This is the implement he uses to rip apart termite nests to get at his favorite food.

Deo rushed up and called the dogs away from the *graman kapasie*. It stood there looking at us, we looked at it, and both wondered what next.

The armadillo came to a decision first. He took off—straight through a patch of *baboenefi* (named for a Hindustani knife), and that was my first experience with *that* stuff, too. This is the famed razor grass or saw grass of tropical and semi-tropical America. It thrives wherever the jungle has been cleared, a harmless-looking, tall, wide-bladed grass growing in patches as innocent-appearing as northern cattail swamps. But each blade sports minute, razory teeth running along the edges.

The giant armadillo scurried massively into the patch, into an over-grown plot of cleared jungle, obviously an old cassava *gron*. Not having had experience with the stuff before, I plunged after him into what looked like an eight- or nine-foot wall of thick grass. The men, I no-ticed about three seconds later, had stopped. I stopped, too. Quickly. My face and arms were cut as though I had run into a batch of razor blades dangling from strings. In dozens of crimson slivers, blood began oozing from my skin. I stood statuelike as the guys came in, hacking their way with machetes, making a tunnel through the razor grass. Blood was running down into my eyes now, and I noticed my ankles leaking into my tennis shoes. In some places the grass had sliced through my shirt and pants, and little slashings of blood were soaking through. I sent one of the guys back to my boat for the first-aid kit, then washed my face and arms in alcohol. It stung briefly, then was all over; the cuts were so thin they seemed to heal almost immediately—after ten minutes or so, hardly bothering me.

Meanwhile, some of the men and dogs had gone around the *gron*, heading the armadillo off, then surrounding him. By the time I got there, they were at an impasse again. And again the armadillo acted. He started digging, scooping the soft, red lateritic sand away with his snout and with his forefeet, flinging it to the sides in pink splashes. I grabbed onto his long, carrot-shaped tail, but my hands, sore from the *baboenefi*, slipped off. I doubt I could have held anyway, though, so strong was the creature.

"*Tjari* [Get the] *doemie goeni*," I told Sime, who was watching with fascination. I planned to inject tranquilizer into the beast directly. But the armadillo was disappearing from view, going down at about a 45-degree angle. I yelled to Sime to bring back a couple of shovels, too.

By the time he returned—not more than five minutes—all we could see of our mammoth friend was that silly oatmeal-colored tail and a sliver of shell. With gusto, the men began digging in front of him, some twelve feet away. By the time I got the syringe loaded, he had disappeared. Hopefully, they would reach a spot in front of him, and he would break through into the open, where I could nab him with a hypo. I sent Sime back for two more shovels.

Part of the idea worked. We got there first, and the armadillo broke through. But he only poked his snout through, then hastily backed up, and began digging away at a different angle. With increased fury, the four shovelers attacked again at two different points. A half hour later, the snout broke through again, disappeared, and the whole digging process began once more. We dug for that animal until two-thirty in the afternoon, nearly four hours in all. At that time he changed tactics: he began burrowing straight down. We gave up.

Every few days through the next several weeks, I stopped off to check on my gross challenger. The island shriveled, food got sparse, and I knew he was getting hungry, probably becoming weak from the beginnings of starvation. No termites were left, and his substitute diet items —insects, lizards, grubs, certain roots, decaying vegetation—were also getting scarce.

One day four months later the island was only a hundred yards across, and no spot was more than six feet above the water—which meant that the armadillo couldn't dig down very far. With shovels and syringes at the ready, four of us stormed the island. We caught him above ground, snorting and scuffling along looking for food. While the three others grabbed him by the tail and the back of the shell— trying to hold him still but succeeding only in impeding his progress—I plunged the hypodermic into his rear leg muscle, just under the shell. I used the fast-acting solution, shooting in $1\frac{1}{2}$ cubic centimeters. Then I helped hold him back. It should have knocked him cold in five or ten minutes.

A half hour later we were still being dragged around the forest floor. Every so often the beast would start to dig, and we'd flip him over on his back, dodging his built-in cleavers. Then he'd right himself and walk off, the four of us slipping and sliding behind. With forty-five minutes gone, I decided to give him another injection. I stepped up the dose and shot enough in him to stop a horse. Half an hour later we were still skiing. Whenever we let go, he would begin to dig down, and though he could burrow only six feet, I was afraid he might dig to the water table line, there to relax, sleep, and drown.

Finally, he began hauling us with less enthusiasm. He was, in fact, staggering a bit. Then he stumbled, began falling every few steps, and two men could pretty well control him. We led him like a drunken bear to the boat, flipped his hundredweight into it, and three of us sat on him while Wimpy piloted us home. We tried to tie those mean forefeet together, but every time we got close, he'd start slinging them around.

Fortunately the trip to camp was short. There, we called for fresh troops, and by alternately pushing and leading the groggy beast, we guided him to the holding area. He was almost unconscious now; he didn't fight or try to dig but he did continue to walk, round and round, in thirty-foot circles as though sleepwalking. We placed an animal trap in front of him. He walked in, hit the bars on the other end, hooked his claws in them, bent and ripped them apart, and walked out the other side to continue his circular pacing. We led and pushed him to the storage hut. He walked in easily enough, and came out the other end, having battered through the wooden planks.

We couldn't hold him. Despite the fact that night was coming, we decided we had better get him to shore while we could still control him a little. Into the boat again, and under three guys went the armadillo, who should have been stoned hours ago. We headed for the nearest *gwamba loesoe pasi*, the boat path where we had cut trails from the lake back through the treetops to the shore for animal release. He seemed to be coming out of it by then—at least he was becoming more aggressive, slinging those forefeet at us with increased vigor.

Finally, as dusk closed in and we felt he was safe to leave alone, we turned him loose and set off for camp again. We could hear him tipsily stumbling and crashing through the undergrowth as we paddled out through the trees.

We never could seem to be able to give giant armadillos enough of the drug to knock them out. With some of the other animals, though, we had just the opposite trouble. One little peccary, for instance, I remember well, a fellow we found on the same island where we got the giant armadillo. All the peccaries we caught during the operation were of the white-collared variety (*Tayassu tajacu*), the same piglike creature found in the extreme southern United States and all the way south to the bottom of South America. Collared peccaries (also called javalina) once roamed as far north as Arkansas, but American sportsmen have succeeded in wiping them out everywhere except along the southern borders of Texas, New Mexico, and Arizona.

The little peccary on the armadillo island, clad in long, stiff fur of grizzly-gray with a white collar around his neck—sort of like a skinny, long-legged Hampshire hog—was chased by Bally's dogs down into a hole. By the time Deo blocked up the other entrance so the animal couldn't run out, the rest of us had arrived. The guys cleared some brush away from the hole, then with shovels dug down about four feet. The little pig felt his rear end exposed to the world, so he turned around and clacked his tusks at us—two uppers pointing down, two lowers pointing up. When cornered, as this one was, peccaries can be vicious. So rather than try to haul him out full of fight, I fitted my tranquilizer pistol with a low charge of dope—enough to stun him, but not put him out for long.

I aimed at his shoulder and fired. He clacked his tusks a couple more times, then, in less than a minute, flopped down. Wimpy had the Ketch-all pole with the slipknot on the end, and he lowered it down and looped it over the pig's neck, then gently pulled him upward, out of the hole.

I knew something was wrong. The peccary was out cold, hardly moving. I pulled back his lips; his tongue and gums were that awful blue color from lack of oxygen. He wasn't breathing. Stretching the two-foot animal on the ground, I started giving him artificial respiration, pushing on his chest in about the same way I did the monkey. But I saw I was too late. His heart had stopped. He was dead.

The tranquilizer needle was still sticking in him, in his chest. I withdrew it, and only then noticed that instead of using the small-animal, $\frac{5}{8}$-inch needle, I had inadvertently used the $2\frac{1}{2}$-inch size, the largest one, to be used only for the biggest creatures. If I had hit him where I had aimed, though—the shoulder—probably no permanent damage would have been done. But I missed. Instead, I struck him in the forward rib cage, probably piercing either his lung or heart. We buried him where we found him.

I was so careful with the next peccary I didn't even use a tranquilizer.

We came upon this one a few days later, on an island near the other, and because this peccary was a young one—only a foot high and a foot and a half long—three of us were able to chase her, surround her, and grab her. She was cute. And I felt so bad about killing the other one I decided to keep her for a pet. We named her Meena, after one of the men's wives.

Meena was rather slim for a pig (actually peccaries belong to a different family than U.S. pigs), and certainly behaved much better than the pigs I knew back in Massachusetts. When she walked on her thin, delicate legs tipped with shiny little hooves, it was most ladylike. When running—considerably faster than I could—her legs moved in a stiff-legged blur, and when she came trotting across the hard-pan center of the camp, her hooves sounded like a dozen tiny horses.

One of her two favorite activities was grub hunting. Her head tapered conelike to a flat, moist, turned-up nose, the nozzle flattened to the size of the bottom of a glass. This was her shovel. She'd snort and shuffle around camp, digging little ditches and piling up mounds here and there, head down, tiny tail up, revealing her golf-ball-size anus, the contexture and color of a rose.

When you'd walk by, she'd look up at you pig-eyed with a terribly dirty nose and want you to pick her up. And that was her other favorite activity: riding around in someone's arms. If you'd do the ultimate— turn her over on her back like a baby and scratch her belly—she'd show her ecstasy by closing her eyes and grinding those teeth-tusks of hers like castanets.

When I was away for a few hours, or even a few minutes, Meena would come trotting up on my return, clacking her tusks, squeaking, snorting with delight, sighing mightily while she poked at my leg with her ridiculous nose. I'd try to walk away, and she'd step between my legs. In order to save myself from falling, I'd have to pick her up.

Early one morning I awakened to find an ice-cold, very wet, rubbery nose snuffling and pushing into my cheek through the mosquito netting. I opened my eyes and there was Meena somehow having clambered up on the table. She gargled a greeting and indicated that we should bundle. So I lifted the netting and she galomphed in. I was sorry I had given in. She danced up and down on me on those stilleto heels of hers, nuzzling with her nozzle, occasionally fluffing her pillow

—me—with her sharp baby tusks. Snort and chatter her tusks as much as she wanted, that was the last time we shared a bed.

Whenever we left in the morning for the day's hunt, she knew she would be lonely for hours, so she'd try to come along. She was extremely intelligent, as are all peccaries, and she'd try to outwit us. She'd watch for signs that we were leaving, then run down to the boats, climb into one of them, and stand very still in hopes that no one would notice her. We'd pick her up and put her on shore, pull away, and she would swim out to us. Then we'd have to back up again, put her on shore, get really angry in our scolding, and maybe she'd stay there.

After we captured Meena, barely tranquilized, we found that the easiest and most practical method of drugging peccaries was with just the needle, no gun. I'd dig down a burrow until I'd come to the clacking tusks, then, holding the animal tight with a Ketch-all pole, I'd pull him forward, grab him with animal gloves, then zip the needle into his shoulder. Afterward, I'd give the peccary a broad-spectrum antibiotic before letting him go, for prevention of possible infection developing at the point where the tranquilizer needle punctured the skin—for it was impossible to keep the needles sterile. We also used the tropical antiseptic Furacin on animals with superficial wounds. Most of the deer we caught, for example, had one or more subsurface worms, usually embedded in the rib cage. We'd slit the wound, squeeze the grub out, then, with a pliable plastic bottle with a long snout on it, we'd squirt some Furacin into the hole. (And sometimes the Bushnegroes would daub the drug on their foreheads for headaches—logical; look how it healed the animals.)

The drugs were carried along with me in the boat, in what I called my bag of tricks—an old BWIA flight bag. Also inside was a first-aid kit (including boxes of antivenin), a can of beans (invariably rusty), malaria pills, pliers, a plastic raincoat, old cassava, waterproof matches, three fishhooks, and a line in case I got stranded, and extra tranquilizer gun parts.

Probably the most dramatic use of the gun came not long after we had got it, on an island just about to go underwater. We had just taken two deer, half a dozen agoutis and pacas, and a few sloths from the land, using eight boats, with two or three men to a boat. We were put-putting through a pass cut with machetes from the island to the main river course, headed for an animal release point some six miles to the west, when suddenly a cry rang out to the side: *"Tigre-katie! tigre-katie"* (ocelot).

Motors roared as we headed in the direction of the yelling, the boats crashing through the thick growth. When we neared we could see the ocelot in the branches—maybe thirty feet up—running from tree to tree as easily as though on land. I loaded my tranquilizer gun, but didn't even try to shoot; the branches were much too thick.

With Wimpy yelling instructions, the men formed a crescent with their dugouts, forcing the cat to flee through the trees toward the open water. Finally she reached a large tree standing rather by itself on the island's edge. The men paddled up behind her, and, with machetes flailing, dropped the adjacent trees into the water, isolating her.

Still sleek and in good, healthy condition—obviously well fed, probably from eating weakened smaller animals—the ocelet hunched snarling at the men as they began cutting the branches from her tree so I could get a clean shot. Suddenly she leaped at one of them. His partner was watching, and while the ocelot was in midair, he spun the boat with his paddle. She splashed into the water on one side of the boat while her intended victim plunged in on the other. Later he claimed he fell.

Each boat had a cat pole in it, but not a single one was fitted together; no one expected the cat to jump. I couldn't see to fire because the action was on the far side of the tree, and if I didn't smack the trunk with the needle, I'd get one of the men. So by the time cat poles were fitted together, the ocelot, wet, dripping, skinny-looking, and twice as mad as before, had climbed back into the tree.

The guys resumed their branch-cutting then—watchfully—and I took a shot, missed, tried again, missed again, both times because of twigs in the way. Then the cat changed branches. I shot a third round, and the needle hit her in the haunches. She hissed, reached back and swatted the needle away, but it was too late; the drug began to affect her almost immediately. She sat down, then lay down, and with a pitiful mew, lowered her head to the branch and went to sleep, her legs dangling on either side. She stayed there, wafting in the breeze like a stole.

Someone *could* go up after her, but because the tree was of softwood, the men decided to cut it down. Again the clang of machetes rang through the area, and soon the tree leaned, cracked, and fell.

As soon as the cat touched the water, she became a splashing, clawing, thrashing mill. She started swimming toward my boat, and, as she approached, I dived into the water, came up beside her, and caught her around the back. It was the first time I had ever grabbed an ocelot, but in the water it was easy; she seemed like a yard-long, quite-heavy house cat. But I knew enough to beware of those claws.

At the side of the boat, while I was trying to decide what to do with her, she passed out again. Treading water, I lifted her up to Sime, who grabbed her by the scruff of the neck and the tail. He laid her, unconscious, in the boat.

Before sliding her into a carrying bag, we inspected her closely. She was beautiful, about two or three years old, in her prime. She had not a mark on her—no ticks in her soft fur of black, ringlike fused spots against a buff background, no signs of worms.

She opened an eye, and quickly before she knew what was happening, I slipped her into a bag. Then she started struggling. To quiet her, I gave her another injection, right through the canvas. Otherwise she would have ripped the bag, maybe even herself.

When we touched land, we found a log and rested one end on the shore, the other on the side of the boat. Then we slid the ocelot out onto the seat. She lay there like a house cat sunning herself, her tail twitching slightly and her eyelids moving, dreaming. Then, in ten minutes or so, she awoke, slowly sat up, regarded us gravely, and slunk slowly along the log, still groggy. Soon as she touched land, though, all grogginess seemed to disappear. Like an alley cat pursued by a pack of hounds, she bounded off into the jungle, off to where food would be considerably harder to get, but where she would have a good chance for a long life.

# NEW YORK
## JEAN-PAUL SARTRE

I really knew I would like New York, but I thought I'd be able to like it immediately, as I had liked the red brick of Venice and London's massive, somber houses. I didn't know that, for the newly arrived European, there was a "New York sickness," like sea-sickness, air-sickness and mountain-sickness.

At midnight, an official bus took me from La Guardia Field to the Plaza Hotel. I had pressed my forehead against the window, but had been able to see only red and green lights and dark buildings. The next day, without any transition, I found myself at the corner of 58th Street and Fifth Avenue. I walked for a long time under the icy sky. It was Sunday in January, 1945, a deserted Sunday. I was looking for New York and couldn't find it. The further I progressed along an avenue that seemed coldly mediocre and banal, the further the city seemed to retreat before me, like a ghost town. What I was looking for was probably a European city.

We Europeans live on the myth of the big city that we forged during the nineteenth century. American myths are not ours, and the American city is not our city; it has neither the same character nor the same functions. In Spain, Italy, Germany and France we find circular cities that were originally surrounded by ramparts meant not only to protect the inhabitants against enemy invasion, but also to conceal the inexorable presence of Nature. These cities are, moreover, divided into sections that are similarly round and closed. The piled-up tangle of houses weighs heavily on the soil. They seem to have a natural tendency to draw together, so much so that now and then we have to clear a way through with an axe, as in a virgin forest. Streets run into other streets. Closed at both ends, they do not look as though they lead outside the city. Inside them, you go around in circles. They are more than mere arteries; each one constitutes a social milieu.

You stop along these streets, meet people, drink, eat and linger. On Sundays, you get dressed and take a stroll for the sole pleasure of greeting friends, to see and be seen. These streets are filled with a communal spirit that changes from hour to hour.

Thus, my near-sighted European eyes, slowly venturing out, on the watch for everything, vainly tried to find something to arrest them. Anything at all—a row of houses suddenly barring the way, a street corner, or some old, time-mellowed house. But it was no use. New York is a city for far-sighted people, a city in which you can only "adjust" to infinity. My glance met nothing but space. It slid over blocks of identical houses, with nothing to arrest it; it was about to lose itself in empty space, at the horizon.

Céline has remarked of New York that "it is a vertical city." This is true, but it seemed to me, at first, like a lengthwise city. The traffic that comes to a standstill in the side streets is all-privileged and flows tirelessly down the avenues. How often the taxi-drivers, willing to take passengers from north to south, flatly refuse to take any for the east and west! The side streets have hardly any function other than to mark off the limits of the apartment houses between the avenues. They are cut by the avenues, spread and thrown toward the north. That was why I, a naïve tourist, vainly tried for a long time to find *quartiers*. In France we are surrounded and protected by urban centers; the prosperous districts protect the rich from the poor, and the poor districts protect us from the disdain of the rich, and similarly, the entire city protects us against Nature.

In New York, where the major axes are parallel avenues, I was unable to discover *quartiers* except on Lower Broadway. I could only find filmy atmospheres, longitudinally stretched masses with nothing to mark a beginning or end. I gradually learned to recognize the atmosphere of Third Avenue where, under the shadow of the noisy elevated railway, people meet, smile and chat without even knowing each other; and that Irish bar in which a German, passing by my table, stopped for a minute to say: "Are you French? I'm a Jerry"; the reassuring comfort of the Lexington Avenue shops; the dreary elegance of Park Avenue; the cold luxury and stucco impassiveness of Fifth Avenue; the gay frivolity of Sixth and Seventh Avenues; the food markets on Ninth Avenue; and the No Man's Land of Tenth Avenue. Each avenue wraps its neighboring streets in its own atmosphere, but one street down, you're suddenly plunged into another world. Not far from the palpitating silence of Park Avenue where glide the cars of the lords and masters, I come to First Avenue where the earth is constantly trembling under the passing of trucks. How am I to feel safe on one of those endless "north-south" highways when, a few steps away to the east or west, other lengthwise worlds await me? Behind the Waldorf-Astoria and the blue and white canopies of "smart" buildings, I glimpse the "Elevated," which carries with it something of the Bowery's poverty.

All of New York is striped this way with parallel and noncommunicating significances. These long, perfectly straight lines suddenly gave me the feeling of space. Our cities are constructed to protect us against it; the houses cluster like sheep. But space crosses through New York, quickening and expanding it. The space, the great, empty space of the steppes and pampas, flows through New York's arteries like a draft of cold air, separating one side from the other. An American friend who was showing me about the smart sections of Boston pointed to the left of a boulevard and said, "The 'nice' people live there." And then, pointing to the right side, he added ironically, "No one has ever been able to find out who lives here." The same is true of New York; between the two sides of a given street, you have all of space.

New York is half-way between a pedestrian's and a driver's city. You do not go for walks in New York; you fly through it; it is a city in motion. I feel at ease if I walk quickly; if I stop, I get flustered and wonder, "Why am I in this street rather than in one of the hundreds of others like it?" Why am I standing in front of this drugstore, or this Schrafft's or Woolworth branch, rather than in front of any other of these thousands of identical ones?

And suddenly pure space looms into view. I imagine that if a triangle could become conscious of its position in space, it would be terrified at the realization of the rigorousness of its defining co-ordinates, but that it would also be terrified to discover that it is merely any triangle, any place. You never lose your way in New York; one glance is enough for you to get your bearings; you are on the East Side, at the corner of 52nd Street and Lexington Avenue. But this spacial precision is not accompanied by any precision of feeling. In the numerical anonymity of the streets and avenues, I am simply anybody, anywhere. No matter where I may be, my position is marked out in longitude and latitude.

But no valid reason justifies my presence in this place rather than in any other, since this one is so like another. You never lose your way, and you are always lost.

Is it a city I am lost in, or is it Nature? New York is no protection against Nature's violence. It is an open-skied city. Storms flood its wide streets that take so long to cross when it rains. Hurricanes shake the brick houses and rock the skyscrapers. They are announced formally over the radio, like declarations of war. In summer, the air vibrates between the houses; in winter, the city is flooded, so that you might think yourself in some Parisian suburb flooded by the Seine, but in America, it is only melting snow.

Nature weighs so heavily on New York that this most modern of cities is also the dirtiest. From my window I see thick, muddy papers, tossed by the wind, flitting over the pavement. When I go out, I walk in a blackish snow, a sort of puffy crust the same color as the sidewalk, so that it looks as if the sidewalk itself is buckling. From the first of May, the heat crashes down on the city like an atomic bomb. The heat is Evil. People go up to one another and say, "It's murder!" The trains carry off millions of fleeing city-dwellers who, on descending from the train, leave damp marks on the seat, like snails. It is not the city they are fleeing, but Nature. Even in the depths of my apartment, I am open to attack from a mysterious and secretly hostile Nature. I feel as though I were camping in the heart of a jungle crawling with insects. There is the wailing of the wind, the electric shocks I get each time I touch a doorbell or shake a friend's hand, the cockroaches that scoot across my kitchen, the elevators that make me nauseous and the inextinguishable thirst that rages in me from morning till night. New York is a colonial city, an outpost. All the hostility and cruelty of Nature are present in this city, the most prodigious monument man has ever erected to himself. It is a light city; its apparent lack of weight surprises most Europeans. In this immense and malevolent space, in this rocky desert that will tolerate no vegetation of any kind, millions of brick, wooden and reinforced concrete houses, that all look as if they are about to fly away, have been constructed.

I like New York. I learned to like it. I become accustomed to its massive groupings and its long vistas. My eyes no longer linger over the façades in quest of a house which might, by some remote chance, not be identical with the others. My eyes immediately slip by to the horizon to look for the buildings lost in fog, mere volumes, merely the sky's austere framework. One is rewarded when one has learned how to look at the two rows of apartment houses which, like cliffs, line a great artery; their mission is completed down there, at the avenue's end, in simple, harmonious lines; a scrap of sky floats between them.

New York reveals itself only at a certain height, a certain distance, and a certain speed; these are not the pedestrian's height, distance or speed. This city looks amazingly like the great plains of Andalusia— monotonous when travelled over on foot, magnificent and changing when seen from a car.

I learned to like New York's sky. In European cities where roofs are low, the sky crawls close to the earth and seems tamed. The New York sky is beautiful because the skyscrapers push it back, very far over our heads. Pure and lonely as a wild beast, it guards and watches over the city. And it is not only a local protection; one feels that it stretches out into the distance over all America; it is the whole world's sky.

I learned to like Manhattan's avenues. They are not sober little walks closed in between houses, but national highways. The moment you set foot on one of them, you understand that it has to go on to Boston or Chicago. It fades away outside the city and the eye can almost follow it into the country. A wild sky over parallel rails, that, more than anything else, is New York. When you are at the heart of this city, you are at the heart of Nature.

I had to get used to it, but now that I have, there is no place in which I feel more free than in the New York crowds. This light, ephemeral city that looks every morning and evening, under the sun's inquisitive rays, like a simple juxtaposition of rectangular parallel-epipeds, is never oppressing or depressing. You can experience the anguish of solitude here, but never that of oppression.

In Europe, we become attached to a neighborhood, to a cluster of houses or a street-corner, and we are no longer free. But hardly have you plunged into New York than your life is completely cut to New York's size. You can gaze down in the evening from the top of the Queensborough Bridge, in the morning from New Jersey, at noon from the seventy-seventh storey of Rockefeller Center, but you will never be captivated by any of the city's streets, because none of them has a distinctive beauty of its own. There is beauty in all of them, as all of America's nature and sky is present in them. Nowhere will you ever have a stronger feeling of the simultaneity of human lives.

New York moves Europeans in spite of its austerity. Of course, we have learned to love our old cities, but their touching quality for us lies in a Roman wall that forms part of an inn's façade, or a house that Cervantes lived in, or the Place des Vosges, or the town hall at Rouen. We like museum-cities, and all our cities are rather like museums in which we wander about amidst ancestral homes. New York is not a museum-city, yet, for Frenchmen of my generation, it already possesses a melancholy of the past. When we were twenty, around 1925, we heard about the skyscrapers. For us they symbolized America's fabulous prosperity. We discovered them with amazement in the films. They were the architecture of the future, just as the cinema was the art of the future and jazz the music of the future. Today we know what to think about jazz. We know that it has more of a past than a future. It is a music of popular, Negro inspiration, capable of limited development and in a process of slow decline. Jazz is outliving its day. The talking film has not fulfilled the promise of the silent one. Hollywood is making no headway in a well-worn rut.

The man who walked about in New York before 1930 saw in the big buildings that dominated the city the first signs of an architecture destined to radiate over the whole country. The skyscrapers were alive then. Today, for a Frenchman arriving from Europe, they are already mere historical monuments, relics of a bygone age. They still rear up against the sky, but my mind is no longer with them, and the New Yorkers pass by at their feet without even looking. I cannot think of them without a certain sadness; they tell of an age in which we thought that the very last war had just ended and when we believed in peace. They are already a bit rundown; tomorrow, perhaps, they will be torn down. In any case, their construction required a faith we no longer have.

I walk between the little brick houses the color of dried blood. They are younger than Europe's houses, but their fragility makes them look much older. Far away I see the Empire State or the Chrysler Building reaching vainly toward the sky, and suddenly I think that New York is about to acquire a History and that it already possesses its ruins.

**JEAN-PAUL SARTRE**

That is enough to lend a bit of softness to the world's harshest city.

# COLD, HURT, AND SORROW:
# STREETS OF DESPAIR
## LEROI JONES

These streets stretch from one end of America to the other and connect like a maze from which very few can fully escape. Despair sits on this country in most places like a charm, but there is a special gray death that loiters in the streets of an urban Negro slum. And the men who walk those streets, tracing and retracing their steps to some hopeless job or a pitiful rooming house or apartment or furnished room, sometimes stagger under the weight of that gray, humiliated because it is not even "real."

Sometimes walking along among the ruined shacks and lives of the worst Harlem slum, there is a feeling that just around the next corner you'll find yourself in South Chicago or South Philadelphia, maybe even Newark's Third Ward. In these places life, and its possibility, has been distorted almost identically. And the distortion is as old as its sources: the fear, frustration, and hatred that Negroes have always been heir to in America. It is just that in the cities, which were once the black man's twentieth century "Jordan," *promise* is a dying bitch with rotting eyes. And the stink of her dying is a deadly killing fume.

The blues singers know all this. They knew before they got to the cities. "I'd rather drink muddy water, sleep in a hollow log, than be in New York City treated like a dirty dog." And when they arrived, in those various cities, it was much worse than even they had imagined. The city blues singers are still running all that down. Specifically, it's what a man once named for me unnatural adversity. It is social, it is economic, it is cultural and historical. Some of its products are emotional and psychological; some are even artistic, as if Negroes suffered better than anyone else. But it's hard enough to be a human being under any circumstances, but when there is an entire civilization determined to stop you from being one, things get a little more desperately complicated. What do you do then?

You can stand in doorways late nights and hit people in the head.

You can go to church Saturday nights and Sundays and three or four times during the week. You can stick a needle in your arm four or five times a day, and bolster the economy. You can buy charms and herbs and roots, or wear your hat backwards to keep things from getting worse. You can drink till screaming is not loud enough, and the coldest night is all right to sleep outside in. You can buy a big car . . . if the deal goes down. There's so much, then, you can do, to yourself, or to somebody else. Another man sings, "I'm drinkin' t.n.t., I'm smokin' dynamite, I hope some screwball starts a fight."

One can never talk about Harlem in purely social terms, though there are ghetto facts that make any honest man shudder. It is the tone, the quality of suffering each man knows as his own that finally

must be important, but this is the most difficult thing to get to. (There are about twenty young people from one small Southern town, all friends, all living within the same few blocks of the black city, all of whom are junkies, communally hooked. What kind of statistic is *that?* And what can you say when you read it?)

The old folks kept singing, there will be a better day . . . or, the sun's gonna shine in my back door some day . . . or, I've had my fun if I don't get well no more. What did they want? What would that sun turn out to be?

Hope is a delicate suffering. Its waste products vary, but most of them are meaningful. And as a cat named Mean William once said, can you be glad, if you've never been sad?

# A PINE CONE, A TOY SHEEP...
## PABLO NERUDA

I'll tell you a story about birds. On Lake Budi some years ago, they were hunting down the swans without mercy. The procedure was to approach them stealthily in little boats and then rapidly—very rapidly— row into their midst. Swans like albatrosses have difficulty in flying; they must skim the surface of the water at a run. In the first phase of their flight they raise their big wings with great effort. It is then that they can be seized; a few blows with a bludgeon finish them off.

Someone made me a present of a swan: more dead than alive. It was of a marvelous species I have never seen anywhere else in the world: a black-throated swan—a snow boat with a neck packed, as it were, into a tight stocking of black silk. Orange-beaked, red-eyed.

This happened near the sea, in Puerto Saavedra, Imperial del Sur.

They brought it to me half-dead. I bathed its wounds and pressed little pellets of bread and fish into its throat; but nothing stayed down. Nevertheless the wounds slowly healed, and the swan came to regard me as a friend. At the same time, it was apparent to me that the bird was wasting away with nostalgia. So, cradling the heavy burden in my arms through the streets, I carried it down to the river. It paddled a few strokes, very close to me. I had hoped it might learn how to fish for itself, and pointed to some pebbles far below, where they flashed in the sand like the silvery fish of the South. The swan looked at them remotely, sad-eyed.

For the next twenty days or more, day after day, I carried the bird to the river and toiled back with it to my house. It was almost as large as I was. One afternoon it seemed more abstracted than usual, swimming very close and ignoring the lure of the insects with which I tried vainly to tempt it to fish again. It became very quiet; so I lifted it into my arms to carry it home again. It was breast high, when I suddenly felt a great ribbon unfurl, like a black arm encircling my face: it was the big coil of the neck, dropping down.

It was then that I learned swans do not sing at their death, if they die of grief.

I have said little about my poems. I know very little about such things, really. I prefer instead to move among the evocations of my childhood. Perhaps, out of these plants and these solitudes and this violent life come the truths and the secret things—the profoundest *Poetics* of all, unknown because no one has written them down. We come upon poetry a step at a time, among the beings and things of this world: nothing is taken away without adding to the sum of all that exists in a blind extension of love.

Once, looking for little trophies and creaturely things of my world in the back of our house in Temuco, I came on a knothole in a neighboring fence post. I peered through the opening and saw a plot very like our own, all wilderness and waste. I withdrew a few steps, with the vague sense of portents to come. Suddenly a hand appeared—the tiny hand of a child just my age. I came closer, and the hand disappeared; in its place was a lovely white sheep—a toy sheep of nondescript wool. The wheels had fallen away—but that only made it more lifelike. I have never seen a more ravishing animal. I peered through the knothole, but the child was nowhere in sight. I went back to the house and returned with a prize of my own which I left in the very same spot: a pine cone I treasured above all things, half-open, balsamic, sweet-smelling. I left it there and I went away with the little toy sheep. . .

# NOTES ON PHOTOGRAPHY

There is a terrible truthfulness about photography.
The ordinary academician gets hold of a pretty model,
paints her as well as he can, calls her Juliet,
and puts a nice verse from Shakespeare underneath,
and the picture is admired beyond measure.
The photographer finds the same pretty girl,
he dresses her up and photographs her, and calls her Juliet,
but somehow it is no good—it is still Miss Wilkins, the model.
It is too true to be Juliet.

**GEORGE BERNARD SHAW**

---

The painters have no copyright on modern art! . . . I believe in, and
make no apologies for, photography: it is the most important graphic
medium of our day. It does not have to be, indeed cannot be—com-
pared to painting—it has different means and aims.

*Whenever I can feel a Bach fugue in my work I know I have arrived.*

**EDWARD WESTON**

---

Of all forms of expression, photography is the only one which seizes the instant in its flight. We look for the evanescent, the irreplaceable; this is our constant concern, and therefore one of the characteristics of our craft. A writer has time to let phrases form themselves before he commits them to paper; he can make an interplay of varying elements; whereas we, once we are back home, can do nothing more about our reportage.

**HENRI CARTIER-BRESSON**

Photography is a medium, a language, through which I might come to experience directly, live more closely with, the interaction between myself and nature.

Reflections of suns and moons and stars! Unfortunately, this is as close as I can get to the actual subjects, although at times I believe I can catch the reflections in my mind's eye. It is interesting that I can find in nature, by the way I look at it, the material to manifest in photographs my inner reflections.

Seeing things in nature radiate a being of their own is important to me. How can one do this unless one really loves? All good art, if seen and perceived simply and openly (without prejudice or preference), gives us the chance to experience this sense of otherness within the physical thing.

**PAUL CAPONIGRO**

---

For in the immediate world, everything is to be discerned, for him who can discern it, and centrally and simply, without either dissection into science, or digestion into art, but with the whole of consciousness, seeking to perceive it as it stands: so that the aspect of a street in sunlight can roar in the heart of itself as a symphony, perhaps as no symphony can: and all of consciousness is shifted from the imagined, the revisive, to the effort to perceive simply the cruel radiance of what is.

*This is why the camera seems to me, next to unassisted and weaponless consciousness, the central instrument of our time.*

**JAMES AGEE**

# CONSERVATION IS NOT ENOUGH
## JOSEPH WOOD KRUTCH

Suppose I began by saying that the more thickly populated an area is, the fewer animals other than man will be found to be living there. No doubt I should be told not to waste my reader's time by telling him that. But the truth of the matter is that the statement would be false or questionable at best.

Consider for example a few square blocks in one of the most densely populated sections of New York City. There are, to be sure, probably fewer insects and worms below the surface of the soil than in the country. But if you count the rats, the mice, the cockroaches, the flies, the fleas, the bedbugs and the whatnots, the chances are that the non-human population above ground would be much greater than it is in most wild areas of equal extent. Even in the streets and in the air above there might well be more English sparrows than there are of all kinds of birds put together in a woodland-bordered meadow.

What we will have to say if we want to be truthful is something more like this: As man moves in, the larger, more conspicuous and, usually, the most attractive animals begin to disappear. Either they "take to the hills," go into hiding, or are exterminated in one way or another. What remain, and often prodigiously increase, are the creatures which either escape attention or find in the filth which crowds of men bring with them a rich pasture.

Even in a region as thinly populated by man as the Sonoran Desert, this law began long ago to operate. There are still a good many of the larger animals to be found if one looks for them in the right places. But they are both fewer and more wary than they were not so long ago. For them the problem of how to live in the desert was complicated by a new factor when man put in an appearance, and the technique which often becomes most completely indispensable reduces itself to one general principle: Keep out of his way. Moreover, the cover of darkness becomes more and more important and some, like the deer, which were once not nocturnal at all tend to become largely so. To find even the larger remaining animals the naturalist with the most benign intentions is compelled to act like a hunter and stalk his game.

A human community thus becomes a sort of sieve with the fineness of the mesh depending upon the thickness of the population. Just where I live, ten or twelve miles from Tucson, you might call the mesh "medium coarse." Jack rabbits as well as cottontails often come almost to my door and are pretty certain to spring up whenever one walks a few hundred yards toward the mountains. There are ground squirrel burrows all about, pack rats here and there and an occasional rock squirrel—a pepper-and-salt-colored creature about the size of an eastern gray squirrel but with a bushy tail which he always carries behind him instead of in orthodox squirrel fashion. Infrequently I hear at night the yipping of a coyote and on at least one occasion I have had to get porcupine quills out of the nose of a neighbor's dog. But all the larger, more spectacular mammals have been screened out, probably within the last decade. Double the distance from town and you may see deer crossing the road. Go twenty-five miles away to a forest ranger's cabin and the ring-tailed cats as well as the foxes sneak up for table scraps. There are even more surprising animals in the rugged area of recent volcanic mountains just west of town. But they have to be looked for.

Though I have never seen a mountain lion in the wild, they are quite common in some of the more mountainous regions of Arizona and one was shot not long ago thirty or forty miles away from here. Bobcats roam wild, if very wary, even closer at hand. A week or two ago I sat for a few hours in a photographer's blind beside a small man-made water hole about fifteen miles from town. First came a buck and a doe who stood guard while their fawn took a long drink, then the curious little spotted skunk and, finally, two of the wild pigs or peccaries locally known as javelinas. At such a moment one feels that even this close to a city there is some wilderness left. But if the city continues to grow it will probably not be left much longer. Deer and javelinas adapted themselves quite happily to the saguaro forest, nibbling the smaller cacti and browsing on the fruit and leaves of desert shrubs. Mountain lions and bobcats kept the population within reasonable limits without exterminating it. But for the larger mammals the question of how to live in the desert tends to become unanswerable when the desert is inhabited by man.

Some of us might be better reconciled to this fact if the war to the death between man and the creatures whom he is dispossessing really was necessary to man's own success. But much of the war is not and sometimes it actually militates against him. To protect his sheep and cattle, the rancher tries to destroy all the mountain lions and bobcats. He comes so near succeeding that the coyote population grows larger. He then enlists government aid to poison the coyotes and when the coyotes are almost eliminated the ground squirrels and the gophers, on which the coyotes fed, begin to get out of hand.

Somewhat belatedly, certain ranchers are beginning to talk about protecting the coyote. If they ever get around to it they will probably, in time, have to begin protecting the mountain lion also. But by that time it probably will be too late. If they had only been content to be a little less thorough in the first place, we might all, including the wild creatures, be better off. And a natural balance is pleasanter than an artifical one, even when the artificial can be made to work.

That this is no mere sentimentalist's fancy is attested by the fact that at least one ranchers' association representing more than 200,000 acres in Colorado has recently posted its land to forbid the killing of coyotes and taken as strong a stand on the whole matter. "We ranchers in the vicinity of Toponas, Colorado . . . are also opposed to the widespread destruction of weasels, hawks, eagles, skunks, foxes and other predatory animals. . . The reason for this attitude is that for ten years or so we have watched the steady increase of mice, gophers, moles, rabbits and other rodents. Now we are at a point where these animals take up one-third of our hay crop. . . What with government hunters and government poison . . . the coyote is nearly extinct in our part of the state. Foxes and bobcats have succumbed to the chain-killing poisons, etc. . . . This spring rodents have even killed sagebrush and quaking aspen trees . . . serious erosion is taking place."

Yet at last report the government was still setting cyanide gas guns and developing the "chain-poisoning" technique which involves killing animals with a poison that renders their carcasses deadly to the scavengers which eat them. And in Arizona the bounty on mountain lions continues.

Moralists often blame races and nations because they have never learned how to live and let live. In our time we seem to have been increasingly aware how persistently and brutally groups of men undertake to eliminate one another. But it is not only the members of his own kind that man seems to want to push off the earth. When he moves in, nearly everything else suffers from his intrusion—sometimes because he wants the space they occupy and the food they eat, but often simply because when he sees a creature not of his kind or a man not of his race his first inpulse is "kill it."

Hence it is that even in the desert, where space is cheaper than in most places, the wild life grows scarcer and more secretive as the human population grows. The coyote howls further and further off. The deer seek closer and closer cover. To almost everything except man the smell of humanity is the most repulsive of all odors, the sight of man the most terrifying of all sights. Biologists call some animals "cryptozoic," that is to say "leading hidden lives." But as the human population increases most animals develop, as the deer has been developing, cryptozoic habits. Even now there are more of them around than we realize. They see us when we do not see them—because they have seen us first. Albert Schweitzer remarks somewhere that we owe kindness even to an insect when we can afford to show it, just because we ought to do something to make up for all the cruelties, necessary as well as unnecessary, which we have inflicted upon almost the whole of animate creation.

Probably not one man in ten is capable of understanding such moral and aesthetic consideration, much less of permitting his conduct to be guided by them. But perhaps twice as many, though still far from a majority, are beginning to realize that the reckless laying waste of the earth has practical consequences. They are at least beginning to hear about "conservation," though they are not even dimly aware of any connection between it and a large morality and are very unlikely to suppose that "conservation" does or could mean anything more than looking after their own welfare.

Hardly more than two generations ago Americans first woke up to the fact that their land was not inexhaustible. Every year since then more and more has been said, and at least a little more has been done about "conserving resources" about "rational use" and about such reconstruction as seemed possible. Scientists have studied the problem, public works have been undertaken, laws passed. Yet everybody knows that the using up still goes on, perhaps not so fast nor so recklessly as once it did, but unmistakably nevertheless. And there is nowhere that it goes on more nakedly, more persistently or with a fuller realization of what is happening than in the desert regions where the margin to be used up is narrower.

First, more and more cattle were set to grazing and overgrazing the land from which the scanty rainfall now ran off even more rapidly than before. More outrageously still, large areas of desert shrub were rooted up to make way for cotton and other crops watered by wells tapping underground pools of water which are demonstrably shrinking fast. These pools represent years of accumulation not now being replenished and are exhaustible exactly as an oil well is exhaustible. Everyone knows that they will give out before long, very soon, in fact, if the number of wells continues to increase as it has been increasing. Soon dust bowls will be where was once a sparse but healthy desert, and man, having uprooted, slaughtered or driven away everything which lived healthily and normally there, will himself either abandon the country or die. There are places where the creosote bush is a more useful plant than cotton.

To the question why men will do or are permitted to do such things there are many answers. Some speak of population pressures, some more brutally of unconquerable human greed. Some despair; some hope that more education and more public works will, in the long run, prove effective. But is there, perhaps, something more, something different, which is indispensable? Is there some missing link in the chain of education, law and public works? Is there not something lacking without which none of these is sufficient?

After a lifetime spent in forestry, wild-life management and conservation of one kind or another, after such a lifetime during which he nevertheless saw his country slip two steps backward for every one it took forward, the late Aldo Leopold pondered the question and came up with an unusual answer which many people would dismiss as "sentimental" and be surprised to hear from a "practical" scientific man. His article, in the *Journal of Forestry*, was given the seemingly neutral but actually very significant title "The Land Ethic."

This is a subtle and original essay full of ideas never so clearly expressed before and seminal in the sense that each might easily grow into a separate treatise. Yet the conclusion reached can be simply stated. Something *is* lacking and because of that lack education, law and public works fail to accomplish what they hope to accomplish. Without that something, the high-minded impulse to educate, to legislate and to manage become as sounding brass and tinkling cymbals. And the thing which is missing is love, some feeling for, as well as some understanding of, the inclusive community of rocks and soils, plants and animals, of which we are a part.

It is not, to put Mr. Leopold's thought in different words, enough to be enlightenedly selfish in our dealings with the land. That means, of course, that it is not enough for the farmer to want to get the most out of his farm and the lumberer to get the most out of his forest without considering agriculture and wood production as a whole both now and in the future. But it also means more than that. In the first place enlightened selfishness cannot be enough because enlightened selfishness cannot possibly be extended to include remote posterity. It may include the children, perhaps, and grandchildren, possibly, but it cannot be extended much beyond that because the very idea of "self" cannot be stretched much further. Some purely ethical considerations must operate, if anything does. Yet even that is not all. The wisest, the most enlightened, the most remotely long-seeing exploitation of resources is not enough, for the simple reason that the whole concept of exploitation is so false and so limited that in the end it will defeat itself and the earth will have been plundered no matter how scientifically and far-seeingly the plundering has been done.

To live healthily and successfully on the land we must also live with it. We must be part not only of the human community, but of the whole community; we must acknowledge some sort of oneness not only with our neighbors, our countrymen and our civilization but also some respect for the natural as well as for the man-made community. Ours is not only "one world" in the sense usually implied by that term. It is also "one earth." Without some acknowledgment of that fact, men can no more live successfully than they can if they refuse to admit the political and economic interdependency of the various sections of the civilized world. It is not a sentimental but a grimly literal fact that unless we share this terrestrial globe with creatures other than ourselves, we shall not be able to live on it for long.

You may, if you like, think of this as a moral law. But if you are skeptical about moral laws, you cannot escape the fact that it has its factual, scientific aspect. Every day the science of ecology is making clearer the factual aspect as it demonstrates those more and more remote interdependencies which, no matter how remote they are, are crucial even for us.

Before even the most obvious aspects of the balance of nature had been recognized, a greedy, self-centered mankind naïvely divided plants into the useful and the useless. In the same way it divided animals into those which were either domestic on the one hand or "game" on the other, and the "vermin" which ought to be destroyed. That was the day when extermination of whole species was taken as a matter of course and random introductions which usually proved to be either complete failures or all too successful were everywhere being made. Soon, however, it became evident enough that to rid the world of vermin and to stock it with nothing but useful organisms was at least not a simple task—if you assume that "useful" means simply "immediately useful to man."

Yet even to this day the *ideal* remains the same for most people. They may know, or at least they may have been told, that what looks like the useless is often remotely but demonstrably essential. Out in this desert country they may see the land being rendered useless by overuse. They may even have heard how, when the mountain lion is killed off, the deer multiply; how, when the deer multiply, the new growth of trees and shrubs is eaten away; and how, when the hills are denuded, a farm or a section of grazing land many miles away is washed into gulleys and made incapable of supporting either man or any other of the large animals. They may even have heard how the wonderful new insecticides proved so effective that fish and birds died of starvation; how on at least one Pacific island insects had to be reintroduced to pollinate the crops; how when you kill off almost completely a destructive pest, you run the risk of starving out everything which preys upon it and thus run the risk that the pest itself will stage an overwhelming comeback because its natural enemies are no more. Yet, knowing all this and much more, their dream is still the dream that an earth for man's use only can be created if only we learn more and scheme more effectively. They still hope that nature's scheme of checks and balances which provides for a varied population, which stubbornly refuses to scheme only from man's point of view and cherishes the weeds and "vermin" as presistently as she cherishes him, can be replaced by a scheme of his own devising. Ultimately they hope they can beat the game. But the more the ecologist learns, the less likely it seems that man can in the long run do anything of the sort.

"Nature's social union" is by no means the purely gentle thing which Burns imagined. In fact it is a balance, with all the stress and conflict which the word implies. In this sense it is not a "social union" at all. But it is, nevertheless, a workable, seesawing balance. And when it ceases to seesaw, there is trouble ahead for whatever is on the end that stays up, as well as for those on the end which went down.

Thus, for every creature there is a paradox at the heart of the necessary "struggle for existence" and the paradox is simply this: Neither man nor any other animal can afford to triumph in that struggle too completely. Unconditional surrender is a self-defeating formula—even in the war against insect pests. To the victor belong the spoils in nature also, but for a time only. When there are no more spoils to be consumed, the victor dies. That is believed by some to be what happened to the dominant carnivorous dinosaurs many millions of years ago. They became too dominant and presently there was nothing left to dominate—or to eat. It is certainly what happens to other creatures like the too-protected deer in a national forest who multiply so successfully that their herds can no longer be fed, or, more spectacularly, like the lemmings who head desperately toward a new area to be exploited and end in the cold waters of the North Sea because that area does not exist.

Curiously, the too tender-minded dreamed a dream more attractive than that of the ruthless exploiters but no less unrealizable. They dreamed of "refuges" and "sanctuaries" where the "innocent" creatures might live in a perpetually peaceful paradise untroubled by such "evil" creatures as the fox and the hawk. But it required few experiments with such utopias to demonstrate that they will not work. A partridge covey or a deer herd which is not thinned by predators soon eats itself into stravation and suffers also from less obvious maladjustments. The overaged and the weaklings, who would have fallen first victims to their carnivorous enemies, survive to weaken the stock, and as overpopulation increases, the whole community becomes affected by some sort of nervous tension—"shock" the ecologists call it—analogous to that which afflicts human beings crowded into congested areas.

No more striking evidence of this fact can be found than what happened when it was decided to "protect" the deer on the Kaibab Plateau in the Grand Canyon region. At the beginning of this century there was a population of about 4000 occupying some 127,000 acres. Over a period of years the mountain lions, wolves and coyotes which lived at its expense were pretty well exterminated. By 1924 the 4000 had become 100,000 and then calamity struck. In one year, 1924, 60,000 victims of starvation and disease disappeared and then, year by year, though at a decreasing rate, the population dwindled.

Wild creatures need their enemies as well as their friends. The red tooth and red claw are not the whole story but they are part of it, and the park superintendent with his gun "scientifically" redressing the balance is a poor but necessary substitute for the balance which the ages have established. We may find nature's plan cruel but we cannot get away from it entirely. The lion and the lamb will not—they simply cannot—lie down together, but they are essential to one another nonetheless. And the lesson to be learned is applicable far outside the field of conservation. It is that though the laws of nature may be mitigated, though their mitigation constitutes civilization, they cannot be abolished altogether.

So far as the problem is only that of the Kaibab deer, one common solution is the "open season" when man himself is encouraged to turn predator and hunters are permitted, as some conservationists put it, to "harvest the crop." To some this seems a repellent procedure and even as a practical solution it is far from ideal. Other beasts of prey destroy first the senile and the weaklings; man, if he selects at all, selects the mature and the vigorous for slaughter. The objection to this method is much the same as it would be to a proposal that we should attack the problem of human population by declaring an annual open season on all between the ages of eighteen and thirty-five. That is, of course, precisely what we do when a war is declared, and there are those who believe that the ultimate cause of wars is actually, though we are not aware of the fact, the overgrazing of our own range and the competition for what remains.

What is commonly called "conservation" will not work in the long run because it is not really conservation at all but rather, disguised by its elaborate scheming, only a more knowledgeable variation of the old idea of a world for man's use only. That idea is unrealizable. But how can man be persuaded to cherish any other ideal unless he can learn to take some interest and some delight in the beauty and variety of the world for its own sake, unless he can see a "value" in a flower blooming or an animal at play, unless he can see some "use" in things not useful?

In our society we pride ourselves upon having reached a point where we condemn an individual whose whole aim in life is to acquire material wealth for himself. But his vulgarity is only one step removed from that of a society which takes no thought for anything except increasing the material wealth of the community itself. In his usual extravagant way Thoreau once said: "This curious world which we inhabit is more wonderful than it is convenient; more beautiful than it is useful; it is more to be admired than it is to be used." Perhaps that "more" is beyond what most people could or perhaps ought to be convinced of. But without some realization that "this curious world" is at least beautiful as well as useful, "conservation" is doomed. We must live for something besides making a living. If we do not permit the earth to produce beauty and joy, it will in the end not produce food either.

# TRUNKO THE ELEPHANT
## ART BUCHWALD

The final story concerns not a person but an elephant, the famed Trunko, star of the Bongling Circus, who had entertained children for 20 years. Unfortunately Trunko was getting old and blind and Mr. Bongling announced he would have to be shot.

A syndicated columnist wrote a story about Trunko and said he had arranged with a gamekeeper to take care of the elephant in his retirement. All that was needed was $7000 to make Trunko happy in his final days. He appealed to all those who had ever seen Trunko to send in their contributions as a tribute to the elephant who had devoted so much time to giving pleasure to others.

The reaction was spontaneous. Not $7000 but $25,000 was raised and the syndicated columnist with press photographers and television cameramen showed up at the Bongling Circus to take Trunko away to his retirement.

While the columnist was posing with Trunko and holding up the check that had saved his life, Trunko, whom you remember we said was going blind, knocked over the columnist and stepped on him, killing him in front of the horrified eyes of the millions of television spectators.

When the owner of the circus saw what had happened he immediately made up his mind. He took Trunko back to his cage and had new posters printed which said SEE TRUNKO, THE WILD ELEPHANT WHO KILLED A SYNDICATED COLUMNIST.

Trunko was once again the biggest drawing card of the Bongling Circus and he lived to entertain a new generation of children, dying peacefully in his sleep among the circus people that he had come to know and love.

# List of Illustrations

133 Photograph by William Seabright

134 Photograph by Garry Winogrand

# Acknowledgments (Continued from copyright page)

The Dial Press, Inc.: For "My Dungeon Shook" by James Baldwin. Reprinted from *The Fire Next Time* by James Baldwin. Copyright © 1963, 1962 by James Baldwin.

S. G. Phillips, Inc.: For "New York" from *Literary and Philosophical Essays*, by Jean-Paul Sartre. Copyright 1955 by S. G. Phillips, Inc.

Art Buchwald and HMH Publishing Co., Inc.: For "Trunko the Elephant," which appeared originally in *Playboy* magazine. Copyright © 1962 by HMH Publishing Co., Inc.

Thomas Y. Crowell Company, Inc.: For a selection from *King Solomon's Ring* by Konrad Z. Lorenz. Copyright 1952 by Thomas Y. Crowell, Inc.

Grove Press, Inc.: For a selection from *The Autobiography of Malcolm X*. Copyright © 1964 by Alex Haley and Malcolm X. Copyright © 1965 by Alex Haley and Betty Shabazz.

Harcourt Brace Jovanovich, Inc.: For a selection from *A Walker in the City*, copyright 1951 by Alfred Kazin.

*Mad* Magazine: for "Word Play." Copyright © 1966 by E. C. Publications, Inc.

William Morrow and Company, Inc.: For "Cold, Hurt and Sorrow (Streets of Despair)" from *Home: Social Essays* by LeRoi Jones. Copyright © 1962, 1966 by LeRoi Jones.

Grove Press, Inc., and Ben Belitt: For a selection from "A Pinecone, A Toy Sheep," appearing in *Evergreen Review Reader*.

William Sloane Associates: For "Conservation Is Not Enough," from *The Voice of the Desert* by Joseph Wood Krutch. (Originally appeared in *The American Scholar*.)

Mrs. James Thurber: For "The Dog That Bit People," copyright © 1933, 1961 by James Thurber. From *My Life and Hart Times*, published by Harper and Row, New York.

To all of the publishers, authors, and agents listed above: We are warmly grateful for your courtesy and helpfulness.